Revelations of the Red Pill: How Will Money Change in the NESARA ERA?

Dr. Scott Young

Copyright

ISBN: 9798790064852

The Bible verses are taken from the amazing HCSB (the Holman Christian Standard Bible) with incredible abilities to save notes, read the Greek and Hebrew wording and study the Word. It is available from LifeWay.com, the Apple App store, and the Android app store.

DEDICATION

I want to thank Wendy for being my lover and friend (she happens to be my wife of 29 years too) who critiques all that I write. Wendy played a powerful role in basing this book inside of the Psychology of Grief. As a master's prepared RN, she has more experience than the huge swaths of humanity in understanding grief on a personal and professional level. She will be pioneering in the near future a new path to help others realize the nature of grief as God reveals it to her.

I also would like to thank Silence Dogood, MBA, named Daniel for his keen understanding of NESARA and the underpinnings of the disruption at hand. Nancy Hubbard also played a critical role in helping me understand more of NESARA as well. Eternally grateful to these two!

Lastly, I would like to thank Dario Perla (DarioPerla.com) for his intriguing help in developing the concepts within this book. His assistance was invaluable.

TABLE OF CONTENTS

By Dr. Scott Young

By Dr. Scott Young

1

What Is The Red Pill?

You may be picking this book up in a state of disrepair that you perceive that you won't recover from. Let me assure you that if you have come this far, you're going to make it.

The TV was blaring and the smart phones a signal that will be unmistakable for the rest of your days – *BEEP, BEEP, BEEP, THIS IS AN ACTUAL EMERGENCY.* It will culminate in the global classroom of the nature of the Cabal. You have witnessed the most recognizable figures in the modern world who drive the ship of our destinies. They were sports stars on the grass and hardwood; they were mainstream personalities opining daily upon the supposed nuances of the inner workings of what we were not privy to. The Cabal was also the Hollywood actors you loved in their portrayal of iconic characters bringing you to tears. The political giants elicited strong emotional responses, but reverent requests to cure the ills of our modern experiment of Democracies or Socialists countries. In this book, we will focus on America.

- Q once stated the following on October 30, 2020, in #4942 (8): "This is not about R (Republicans) v D (Democrats); This is about preserving

> our way of life. IF AMERICA falls, the World Falls. Patriots on guard. Q"

By the way, what does Q as a concept mean? It started in late 2017 with a 4chan site then moved to 8chan to improve the message. They (the Q team) had immaculate information with which almost no one could argue. They put out pieces of puzzles of Child Sex Trafficking, Election Fraud and COVID craziness along with the Elite Cabal who were in charge of the narrative. Those phraseologies seems prophetic and almost Biblical (of course it's not Biblical in any shape or form).

Q doesn't mean anything nefarious. The team was put together by government officials with Trump being in charge of the top with Generals who have Q clearance. In the movie "Oppenheimer" a flick about the controversial nature of the man who helped to create the first nuclear weapon in American history, he receives the mythical Q clearance after he is cleared of his Left Leaning Communist ways earlier on in his career. Q clearance then means one who has a military ability to manipulate the nuclear codes or works with the nuclear arsenal of our country.

But this team of Q were giving out cryptic information that didn't seem rational at the time but as the moments moved into months to years, they were never more true than at the time they were written. Therefore, Q isn't just the stuff of legend but a counter-revolutionary idea of generals who hated the Cabal direction of our governments with a long term plan to solve our Electoral, COVID, Child Trafficking Crises of the past and the future direction of the country.

In any case, we must take on what America does as the key to world political health. You may have already learned that NESARA (National Economic Security and Reformation Act) was the progenitor of GESARA (Global), because Trump and the White Hats were behind this transition of which you are now learning. We also must deal with the corruption in America first. The world would be a longer book, so we will not touch that. But, realize that much of the world's brokenness will be solved around the same time that America is.

CONCEPT OF THE RED PILL

The Red Pill has an illustrious story that might surprise you. In *MASH* Season Six, we have an unforgettable episode called *Change Day*. Colonel Potter received a call from ICOR telling him that the military script would be replaced soon. He only allowed Max Klinger in on the secret, although it was an open secret among the camp and the people about their unit within a brief time.

Major Charles Emmerson Winchester decided to capitalize upon the Script Change by giving each South Korean $10 Green American dollars in exchange for each $100 military script provided. Since the Koreans were not allowed in the camp before or after the script was replaced, they had little choice but to grumble over the evil transaction. Many also discovered the dastardly deed of Charles and thwarted his efforts by delaying his entry into the camp. When he arrived, Klinger was in a Navy getup customary for Max, striving to represent his eligibility for a Section Eight discharge from the military. The guards and Klinger informed Major Winchester in no uncertain terms that he was not allowed to enter the camp, and no one would help him replace the old blue script with the red script that would be its value until another change day was initiated. Hence, the *Blue to Red* was all the way back in 1978 when the episode aired.

In the movie trilogy "The Matrix," in the first iteration of the triplet, our main character Neo is given a choice by Morpheus, the heroic character he had only researched who had bucked the system with his daring raids upon the authorities. Morpheus held two gelatinous pills in his hands. Within the left hand was a blue pill that would allow Neo to return to his previous reality and believe a new false narrative. Neo could also have chosen the red pill, allowing him to discover the true nature of their prison. Of course, Neo readily accepted the *Red Pill*, a tracer program designed to find him within the maze patchwork of humanity plugged into a biological process designed to reduce humanity for machines into batteries to feed their power needs.

The Q movement and Patriots worldwide began to adopt this conceptual framework within the realities you are seeing at this very moment. The Cabal's evil inside the Media, Social Media moguls, Central Bankers, Hollywood doing the work of their CIA overlords and the government of the Cabal on both sides of the supposed ideological fence. The Cabal was really Satanists clothed in business suits and trim jowl lines emulating a tailored construct of the faux world in which they were masters of the race. The people of this world have been duped, at least for the past one hundred plus years of this iteration of the Satanists, who diss the God of the universe for one in the underverse that overwhelms the people's pleasure centers (such as sports, movies, pornography and TV streaming).

Q, inside of its military intelligence made up of approximately ten brilliant people, helped those who were or would be awakened to the message that what they believed is the world as they loved it was built in a lie not too dissimilar to *The Matrix* Neo's worldview. Let's move forward to the whys of this illegal and illegitimate organization inside of the history they manipulated.

2
The History of the Cabal

How did you awaken inside of this mess we saw as our world? Ponder the moment you came to your senses. Was it at the Red Pill Event in which you were jolted awake? Did it occur decades ago, as I did slow rousing from my slumber when studying the works of the CIA and its minions in the murder of JFK, Sr. that I began to compile when I was first married in 1993? Or was it in President Trump's first term where you came to a new knowledge that something wasn't right? However, that moment arrived in your heart, your Soul (*psyche* in Greek, which houses your Mind, Will and Emotions and in which we derive the term Psychology; this is the study of the balance of the individual inside the Mind, Will and Emotions) has the innate ability to ask complicated questions far beyond the simple need questions of the Body? The Soul asks: Where am I going in this life? Why is the world operating upside down from my moral framework?

They love to fancy you into the world of sports (my fascination), movies (moved by it as well), internet/gaming, or to the sidelong passions of the political theatre set up in Washington, DC, each four-year term of presidency. But in any of the above instances of your awakening, you have come to know a concordance of new constructs that redefine your world outside the placement of the lies of the Cabal. The Cabal has wound themselves so profoundly inside the walls of the systems we hold dear that they could not easily be extracted. The Great Awakening progenitors formed a think-tank of committed individuals who began their planning since JFK, Senior was murdered on 11/22/1963 on a blustery day in Dallas, Texas.

JFK Killing and the Moniker of the Conspiracy Theorist

The blunderings of George H. Walker Bush during that fateful day in Dallas, then ordered by the CIA to Dallas to lead the multi-corporate killers that included the Mob and Intelligence Agencies, would take decades to understand the sickness of the plan. They comprised a matrix across a broad spectrum of haters for the bold President John F. Kennedy policies he had outlined in a speech to the United Nations only six months earlier in 1963. JFK intoned that a secret cadre of men sought to overthrow America by subversion. JFK also wanted to end the useless Vietnam War and replace our monetary supply back on a Silver Standard inside of the Treasury Department, so that it could not be hijacked further by the secret agencies. He further opined against the Central Intelligence

Agency creating wars that ravaged the world from their own sovereignty to buy political influence and enslave new sectors of populations with their reserves to be plundered.

After JFK was executed in Dealy Plaza that afternoon from a convenient excuse of a poor vantage point behind a grove of trees and high above his target, the blame was penned solely upon Lee Harvey Oswalt. Oswalt had nefarious anti-governmental acquaintances that made him the perfect "patsy," as he wailed being moved from room to room in the Dallas Police Department directly after the killing. Within days of the assassination of the beloved president, Jack Ruby, a local nightclub owner who had potential ties to the Mob of the area, gunned down Oswalt in front of Dallas Police. This assured that Ruby would die in prison for his actions, and the American people would never know the truth within the troubled Oswald.

This critical event in world history is remembered wanly by those alive on that day, just as memorable as 9/11 or the Pearl Harbor Attacks of December 7, 1941. I have spent countless hours investigating this crime of the previous century to endless detail which has awakened me to distrust the government.

But when I visited Dealy Plaza and the Book School Depository in the middle 1990s, scant references to the conspiracy were given to those who might have killed Kennedy instead of or with Oswalt. The governmental officials would only admit that less than 10% of Americans agreed with a conspiracy. But in 2017, when I revisited the site for the sixth time, the museum begrudgingly acceded to the awareness that the vast majority of Americans doubted the bungled evidence of the Warren Commission. Judge Earl Warren headed a chair of Senators and one future president in Gerald Ford, pushing together scenes that ignored massive evidence against the lone gunman, until they derived the lowest confidence theory of "The Magic Bullet."

Inside this pristinely kept bullet (which was suspiciously found upon the gurney of JFK's lifeless body) lies the single shooter evidence that one man committed the crime without help from outside conspirators for the murderous act. The trajectory and velocity changes of the shell were so suspect that no one could duplicate even the entry of the wound from behind, not to mention the course of the pristine casing found on the gurney of JFK's last resting place in Parkland Hospital. Since Oswalt was only a low-level Marksman by military standards of the day, it was highly implausible that he could have accomplished a shot that even expert marksmen couldn't reproduce with any level of consistent accuracy. I will not move into all the inaccuracies and responsiveness of the horrible report called the *Warren Report* that didn't characterize the truth of the day since others do that with more significant levels of justice than I can.

But when you consider the fraudulent nature of the *Magic Bullet* with the severe scrutiny, the fascinating point about the Warren Commission was that when the public pushed back upon the lack of evidence for a single shooter, even to this day, the government hurls the insult created by the CIA called "Conspiracy Theorist." You are deemed a tin-foil hat nutjob who can't get in with the flow of the people of the planet, trying to forge a name for yourself in the idiot annals of history.

That inflammatory phrase against a person creates a back-room secretive tone by the individual uttering the following iconic response: "I don't want to seem like a Conspiracy Theorists, but it doesn't make sense." So instead of the authorities working to debunk your theories, all they pose without the witness of evidence began the death phrase of *Conspiracy Theorist* to marginalize one's concerns. But as you can see with the JFK killing, it is in keeping with the traditional norm does little good to the official position, since no one agrees with it other than the Elite Cabalists.

But this was when the plan for Q was derived by its own reckoning. The White Hats, or the Anti-Cabal as my friend Will used to intone, where the born in the back rooms of military intelligence who hated the lack of freedoms taken away by the Cabal from the people of the world, specifically inside of America. But that's not the beginning of this iteration of the Cabal.

Lincoln, the Civil War, and the Green Back Dollar

One of my favorite presidents was Abraham Lincoln. He was not a perfect man by any means, but he did revere his Creator and fought for the slavery of the black man that their ancestors had not solved in the Constitutional foundations. The Founding Fathers knew that slavery would be a divisive issue, including many of the musings of John Adams and others indicating that it could tear our nation down before it had a chance to start. All of the other civilized countries had already banned the practice of officially taking human slaves as property (this doesn't mention the abhorrent practice we are witnessing by the Cabal in the Sex Slave debauchery). America would have to face the music when the South ceded their states from the North in 1860 that lasted until 1865.

The bloody nature of the Civil War included more Americans per capita than any other war in our history, including the Revolutionary War. The South wanted the autonomy that the North didn't like to offer in choosing its direction of slavery and its economic concerns. Others over the years mention that the war was about State's Rights that had been ignored from the foundation of America almost one hundred years before that bloody conflict. Americans were not prepared for the blatant level of brutality.

In the early days of the war, the towns' people would settle upon a hillside to witness a sight that they would never behold in their wildest dreams, a battle commencing in front of their eyes. But the silly constructs of the bystanders was that the carnage would never spill upon their picnic baskets until it was too late to swoon from the fighting.

However, Lincoln broke many molds and

minds in his contrary Executive Powers. He freed the slaves and allowed them to fight alongside the Northern Units to ultimate victory, even if they weren't granted equal pay or even the basics of respect for their sacrifice. But the Cabal was not as upset by the nature of the Emancipation Proclamation, as they were for the brazen act of authorizing Lincoln's Congress to create its own money, known as the Green Backed Dollar. This was a bridge too far for the Cabal to reconnoiter.

While the war for the South was unwinnable, without outside help from England that they so desperately sought, they fought a series of ragtag battles against completely incompetent generals of the North until they were bested by General Ulysses S. Grant's superior firepower, manpower, and effective tactics against a flagging Southern army who never had the resources to begin with. But when Lincoln commissioned Congress to make its own money through the Treasury in 1863 by passing the National Bank Act. Even though the Greenback Dollar was indebted to the banks, it was sufficiently outside of the Central Banks of the Rothschilds to witness a need to kill the man who formed the idea.

When on April 9th of 1865, we beheld the official surrender of the South with Robert E. Lee signing the documents of the dissolution of the rebellion, all who are students of this war realized it was only a formality on par with Japan's Surrender in 1945 on the Deck of the Missouri. Both nations had lost long before that moment.

Then why would John Wilkes Booth have to kill Lincoln only five days later in the Ford's Theatre in another level of rebellion against the North? If the war was over, why would there be a need to kill this hero of the Republic and then cover the evidence of John Wilkes Booth? There are startling ideas that the government actually killed those conspirators in a barn only a few days later in a horse-collar fire where the criminals would never tell their tale. I postulate that it was more to do with the Central Bank building its future case against those who would oppose their rule. This hypothesis should be further investigated once we recover the documents that really haven't been released to the public along with the Kennedy Assassination.

The Titanic

Few historical events have captured my curiosity as keenly as the Titanic sinking. Most of us know the story in its broad strokes, which I will sketch here. In April 1912, the White Star Line launched its newest and most grand vessel for luxury passage across the Atlantic for those bound to America from Europe.

The Titanic would sail from Ireland to New York City in the early spring which could be dangerous to boats cruising the waters without a careful watch tower of sailors to spot icebergs that might dispossess the passengers of their lives. But Captain Smith, a grizzled veteran of the passage, was sailing confidently across the Atlantic with extreme rapidity and little wind in the newfangled steam engines that allowed impressive speeds to the burgeoning superpower called the United States. It carried a massive group of luxury First Class passengers, including Benjamin Guggenheim, Isa Strauss and John Astor who were millionaires of the time. They could be considered worth eleven billion in today's economy.

With limited lifeboats for the two thousand passengers since the ship was called "Unsinkable," there was no perceived need to waste space with useless lifeboats. But once the vessel was critically wounded on its decks below the water's surface from the jagged ice cap, it was certain to reduce its capacity to massive causalities. More than five hundred people made it to safety even though the boats could be piled with hundreds more to save more than the fifteen hundred who would die.

But what you don't know about this tragedy is that JP Morgan (Chase Morgan Banks of the future) was the owner of the White Star Line. Its sister ship was the Olympic Carrier, damaged in an accident in the same spaces that the Titanic was lost. If a damaged carrier went down in the waters of the Atlantic, the insurance money would only be three million pounds to compensate the Liner company. But if a new one was to sink, the reimbursement would rise to eleven million. Through many sources, it's widely known that the Titanic was switched before its lunch with the Olympic and repainted to look like the Titanic.

JP Morgan canceled his ticket aboard the liner just before its passage. Astor,

Guggenheim, and Strauss were ardent opponents to the Aldrich Act of the previous Congress sessions that failed to bring a Central Bank to America. The new legislation would be termed the Federal Reserve that would bypass to recognition of the people that it had no agency inside the Federal Government to do the will of the elected people of the USA.

With those wealthy passengers out of the way of the Federal Reserve Act, the bill was sent to President Woodrow Wilson's desk to sign on December 23, 1913. He was compelled to do so since he, the Democratic Representative, was backed by the Cabal bankers who pushed this bill forward. Interestingly, the loser Republican candidate Teddy Roosevelt had massive backing by the same Cabal who didn't really care who got into power. They would both do the bidding of the wealthy Elite to control the money. Here we have the largest False Flag event in human history where the Cabal covered up their other crimes with a more significant event.

3
THE FEDERAL RESERVE

Once the Federal Reserve was put in place after the Elite Bankers had their monetary source to control America, they placed themselves in the way of Congress and its ability to control the money for the people. The first goal was to create a debt of the American population to the Cabal bankers. They needed a trigger.

World War One, or the Great War, was also known as the War to End All Wars. It started in Sarajevo, Czechoslovakia, in 1914 when Prince Ferdinand and his young wife were gunned down. Instead of sparking a local rebellion that might have consumed a few nations in its scope, Russia, Germany, Austria, The Ottoman Empire (later Turkey and Iran), England, France, along with the USA, later would create the first modern war of attrition killing more millions than ever was known in the history of warfare. Some estimates were as low as eleven million killed, but I believe more than thirty million perished after my own studies upon that conflict.

WORLD WAR ONE

The importance of this worldwide conflict cannot be overstated to the Cabal bankers already in existence in Europe, with the Rothschild families playing a massive role in creating the Federal Reserve and the banking families of the European continent. They strove to bring countless nations into the war with a cruelty never seen before in battle. In the Ottoman Empire fighting against Russia, young Christian girls were crucified on crosses strewn about the landscape in the thousands only for their religious persuasion to cleanse the land for the Muslim influence to spread to Europe.

It has long been known that both sides of the war were purchasing goods to further the conflict from the Federal Reserve who would exert their influence over the continent with war material to continue the killing of both Hun and French alike. The French and English were losing their touch as world powers sank their fortunes into the war, making them paupers and slaves to the conquering Central Bankers who would require their payment after the war was won. The Germans would pay more dearly than any nation in history.

Woodrow Wilson's health was failing, and his plan to create a League of Nations, the bastion of world countenance to communicate with sovereign nations who didn't see eye to eye, was understood to be the new way of peace on a planet that had more interconnectedness than ever before. Kingdoms morphed into smaller cadres of nations after the war. Germany was made to sign the Versailles Armistice in late 1919 in France, promising to pay for both party's war debt back to the American Bankers who had promulgated the war in the first place. How nice of them, huh?

The Roaring 20s and the Great Depression

Have you ever asked the question about critical events in our history? Why did they happen the way they did? If the answer is no, you will start to change your lack of research as we move forward.

The 1920s, for America at least, was a time of significant expansion on a financial front. Europe was covering the pocked holes that the Great War had wrought. No time in the continent's history, including through the plagues of the Middle Ages, had the landscape been so strewn with bodies needing to be buried. America was booming in more ways than one. For the first time in its history, the finances flowed from Europe because both sides owed them a debt that they could scarcely repay. The Fed knew that they could not but didn't care.

To increase the monetary flow in a high time, the concept of Margins was created for the masses. You could now buy stocks upon the market for 10% of what you could purchase outright. Why pay the total amount? If you dove in on a stock, let's say for fictional sake, of XPF that started at $10 a share, and you wanted 1000 shares, you had a potential of $10,000 in your pocket for the nominal fee of $1000. Of course, that's a substantial chunk for the time, but you would only have to pay back that 90% once you sold it.

As the 1920s breezed by, your XPF stock rose to $30 per share. You were prosperous for the time with $30,000 available with the need to give back your $9000 with an amount left over of $21,000. That's a ton of dough! But there was a nefarious meeting occurring in the backrooms of the Fed that you were unaware of. In February of 1929, the Central Bankers would pull the rug out from underneath you by requiring a Margin Call in October of 1929. Before you knew it, you would be broke.

It's interesting to note that on Valentine's Day 1929, one of the bloodiest assaults in Chicago gangland occurred by Bugs Moran of more than seven rival members. I believe that this was another of the Cabal's False Flag events to cover the nature of the criminal meeting to defraud the public. False Flags have fantastic potential to direct the public's knowledge away from the potential crisis looming and upon a shooting that would capture the nation's outrage and disgust. We see this played out repeatedly as Crisis Actors have done in the late 2010s and beyond.

When Black Tuesday arrived in late October 1929, the world would not sell their precious shares, because there suddenly were only sellers, not buyers. Then the stocks would drop to ridiculous rates until they were in pennies per share, and the Cabal repurchased it from you. You had no way to pay it back. You were destitute without a house or job to back you up. You would now belong to the bread lines of the

1930s, hoping for a job and a bowl of soup to sustain you!

The Stock Market Great Crash of 1929 precipitated the Great Depression, in which billions of dollars would change hands from the ordinary people to the richest of the rich. The superpower of wealth settled into a treasured few pockets. The world would suffer, and the Germans could not pay their people with the worthless currency of the Reich. Their Reich's Mark was brought in wheelbarrows to the local store to be traded in for a loaf of bread due to the first understanding of Hyper-inflation. Does that sound a little familiar to you? Joe Biden began that trend again in 2021.

Gold Stolen in 1933

History hates telling you the details since the victors write the tales you consume. But in 1933, with the Great Depression raging across all countries, Franklin Delano Roosevelt (FDR) chose a curious course of action with our money source. He was required to present all the privately held gold to government officials for the price of $20.60 an ounce. But he stepped the request to a requirement when it had the added teeth of a ten thousand dollar fine for those who didn't turn in their gold. Loud grumblings were heard around the country, but no one could stand against the government's greed for the need to have the gold stored in a vault for the nation's public safety.

Within one year, along with his private advisors, FDR raised the price of gold to a new time high to $33 per ounce once he had all the gold in the storehouses. That means the Fed, who housed the gold for the public safety in 1934, had defrauded the people by reducing the value of their money by a whopping 62%.

In a little more than five years, the Cabal, through its arm of the Fed, had stolen people's pensions, savings, gold, and houses as the Depression showed no signs of letting up. But no one was the wiser. The Federal Reserve became the sword for the Cabal to take control of the money. Let's explain their sick plan.

Path of Your Money to their Pockets, but Who was taking it?

Let's say you pay $10,000 in income taxes per year. Your company dutifully has a payroll company to pull the taxes from your pocket before you ever even smell the greenbacks. It moves from you to the IRS who takes their chunk for their bloated payroll.

Once the IRS is done, the Treasury jumps in the middle of your cash to make it legal inside the Federal Government under the overall provisions of the Constitution. Once they are through with their share, it's earmarked for the Federal Reserve. But who owns the Fed?

All thirteen banking families such as the Rothschilds, Rockefellers, Morgans, and peekaboo...the Queen of England! Yes! They stand to take the next six percent of your cash to disperse for their own needs. Your money begins to work only after your share to pay down the debt.

As of October of 2021, the Federal Reserve holds the nation's debts and all of us hostage to 29 trillion dollars of obligation that counts for more than 400 billion just to pay the interest on the three trillion of potential income tax money given to them. Of course, there is no way to pay down that debt.

When my business failed so miserably in 2009, I was $435K in debt with gross earnings of $509K. That's approximately a 90% debt to income ratio. I didn't know at the time, but either company or person can claim bankruptcy at 30-50% debt to income ratios. I only had $5000 in savings for the company, and I had NO money to run the business and barely paid myself over about a three-year timespan.

The Fed is sitting at a toxic 175% debt to income ratio. On top of that, they are the debt storage of last resort for the country when we are in tough financial times. In 2009, both Freddie Mac and Fannie Mae, horribly run institutions who stole billions from the people in Ponzi schemes in the housing market. They allowed people with terrible credit reports who they knew couldn't make their mortgage payments to get bigger and bigger houses. When they collapsed, the Fed took their debts upon themselves to not go bankrupt and sink the nation fully.

Once the Fed has taken their cut of the above money, it's released to the US Mint who creates the cash, digitally and physically, then moves back into the private sector to be spent again. This is the definition of a Fiat Currency that is only backed by the people's confidence.

Economists greedily preach this message that if people spend, we are all fine.

Over the years, we have seen the Fed kill the economy repeatedly with their False Flags. One of those was the gold stealing of 1933. Again, another momentum shift came in 1971 with the gas shortage covering the petro dollar losing its war with the world. We were paying other nations in gold for our debts. When President Nixon shut off the spickets of gold reserves, the world responded by an oil embargo against us. All we knew was that the pumps were empty.

The Fed is a severe evil run by greedy freaks who worship Satan. Does that go too far in your book? Have you not watched the evidence within the Red Pill? Listen to the “rest of the story,” as Paul Harvey used to say on the radio!

4

THE CABAL STEAL

When I started to research this book, I wanted to get a background on the banking agencies. There is so much garbage that it was hard to wade through. The Securities and Exchange Commission (SEC) is a governmental authority over the banking Cabal we decry in this book. But here's their actual wording, top dead center of their website in the first paragraph "No profession or industry has maintained higher standards of conduct nor provided great public service than the banking industry. Banks have traditionally recognized their duty to act in a manner of public trust and confidence (1)." What? It's as asinine of a statement to purport when CNN, during the Riots of 2020, with burning buildings torched in many Wisconsin cities, saying that the protests are "mostly peaceful." Again, I say what?

When a governmental agency cannot even initiate a position of neutrality in policing the one under their scrutiny, how can we believe them? On a site discussing "Ethical Issues in the Financial Services (2)," the writer brings out four divisions of unethical occurrences within the banking industry:

1. Self-interests sometimes morph into greed

and selfishness.
2. Some people suffer from a stunted moral or legal development in adolescence.
3. Professional duty can conflict with the company's demands.
4. Individual responsibility can wither under the needs of the rich client.

A former head of Wells Fargo was barred from working in the banking industry (3). There are numerous levels of financial crime that never rise to the news levels; why? Because they aren't that sexy to report on. But they are far worse than you realize. Let's give you one of the biggest of this century.

The TARP program of October 2008 was bringing the bankers a boost in the capital when the Great Recession was hitting the world. And why did the Great Recession actually begin? Because mortgage bankers, led by the leading banks, were giving people loans to homes that they clearly could not afford, and what's worse is that those loans were done under just interest payments called an Adjustable-Rate Mortgage (ARM).

Instead of paying any principle, the person could have an ARM applied to their home at $1200 for a typical house payment of $3000. The couple couldn't afford that loan but were told that by the time the actual charge was due, they may have moved out of the house into a better home for them (moving up in the world when they made more money). I remember hearing of this loan type in 2003. Wendy and I looked askance at the Mortgage Broker, telling him that it was stupid. But that's precisely what sunk the Denver Area into people coming up on their ARMs and walking out of the house they could never afford. Hence, the banking crisis was raging in the late 2000s.

Instead of giving needed cash to the people who could rebuild their lives and credit, George W. Bush and his Cabal playmate Barack Obama hatched a scheme where each bank was given more than $250 billion to recover from the crisis. In addition, $68 billion was given over to American International Group (AIG) who couldn't even make payroll (a terrible sign for a business that should declare bankruptcy).

What The Cabal Did and May have done with the Money?

What do we know about the usage of the TARP money? We know that JP Morgan gave 1626 employees at least one million in bonuses that year, and Goldman Sachs gave 953 employees the same (4). What? Instead of dumping in back into the economy to spur loans and potential growth, as is the Fed mandate for those banks, they choose to line their own pockets! But asking the Fed to mandate banks again is like asking the fox to guard the henhouse.

Supposedly, if the government believed in the topic, all the banks paid back their amounts. But from significant financial scuttlebutt in many circles (sorry, but we cannot corroborate even if they received what they say they received), instead of the potential $250 billion given to these Cabal/Central Banks tied to the Fed, they may have received in the tens of trillion-dollar ranges.

My friend, Will, who passed away October 1, 2020, was the progenitor of my economic research. From 2009 to 2013, I endeavored to discover how little I really trusted the Lord about money. I chose to take all the reigns of control, and God allowed me to take the leather straps of control. I felt I was supposed to manage the ship of my debt load, because I had created the mess. My reasoning is familiar to most: why would I allow Jesus to clean up the muddy room when I was the one who tracked in from the slop of the world?

Once I realized that I had to give over my control of the uncontrollable (i.e., debt), God began to mold my mind into a new reality. Sin is mine. Of course, I am the one who did it. But I cannot recover my place with the Father inside the sin forgiveness model Jesus created. But did you realize that the Word for Sin in the New Testament is called *Hamartia?* It also includes debt within its broader definition. I had created the debt, but I didn't have to own it. Revolutionary, I know, but it's also controversial for most Christians who need to "own up to their sin nature." I had done that. But did I have to *own* it, meaning that I keep the sin inside of me along with the nature of the debt to solve it myself? Nope!

Once I had begun to allow the Lord to kill my debt in His timing, I found a freedom I had never known. Then Will started to teach me of his group, the Anti-Cabal representatives, who would fund him down the road for the ministry work he wished to do. It was then I learned that the Anti-Cabal (of whom you would call the White Hats) tried to bring in trillions to America in the form of at least eighty-seven trillion to release the USA from their debts. In 2011, Barack Obama blocked the monetary transfer in The Hague Court, an international response to cross-country disputes. Now, the whole eighty-seven trillion didn't enter America, but a portion did. That's what the Cabal took for itself and never paid it back to the people of whom it was meant.

Once the Anti-Cabal demanded their money back, the Cabal sources in the government and the Fed reported that they would release the funds back to their owners once the Anti-Cabal promised to back Hillary Clinton in her bid to take America into its new destiny in 2016. The Anti-Cabal wanted nothing to do with the Communist plan and bided their time to pounce. Can I corroborate this with other pieces of evidence? These were the reports from several verbal responses. I wish I had the documents. But that will come in time.

Consider though 2023 with the above indicators? Is the Cabal trying to take us into Communism in the form that I had heard back in 2013? That is unquestioned, while God is saying no to the Cabal.

I will not detail Pedophilia, the Satanic Agenda, the Steal of the 2020 Election in this book, and I think we will see all of those in movies to come. Suffice it to say that Hollywood, the Government, Big Tech Firms, and the Media will all pay for their crimes against humanity. Executive Order #13818 (written in the end of 2017 by President Trump) indicated that those who have completed these crimes against humanity cannot transfer their great wealth in any shape or form into the Gold Standard return to a real currency first in America under NESARA and then in the world with GESARA for each country.

9/11 Crime Against Humanity

I will not do historical justice for this criminal event, but I want to reorient what you might know of 9/11. Of course, you will recall that two planes supposedly hit World Trade Center buildings One and Two. They fell within hours in the strangest of circumstances in what was ultimately known as a virtual pull. That means that the buildings collapsed upon themselves in successive destruction of each floor in rapid response to the last floor's explosion. As you doubtless know by now, this is a complete fabrication by George W. Bush, his staff, the media and Hollywood. Building Seven wasn't even hit in the fraudulent airplane strikes; it came down in less than seven seconds. Larry Silverstein, who had re-insured the building only a few weeks earlier with up to $4.1 billion, told a CBS reporter on-air that his building had to be vacated, because it was to be *pulled*, as he explained by phone.

Anyone who researches for a few hours knows that jet fuel doesn't burn hot enough to collapse a building that has been corroborated by multiple engineers and architects worldwide. They were all pre-planned to come down, and a weapon barely even dreamed of called a Directed Energy Weapon (DEW) shot from the sky to destroy the building and almost three thousand people along with it. More fraudulently was how the CIA planned and executed a missile strike against a barely occupied section of the Pentagon. No evidence of an airplane existed from the detailed trails of investigations after the incident.

But why did it all occur? Was it poorly trained Muslims flying into the buildings to kill Americans? You know the truth by now that it was not. Our own CIA pre-planned the attack to galvanize America to shrug off their freedoms inside of the Patriot Act and many other new agencies such as the National Security Agency (NSA) that didn't have to exist. The government wanted to spy on your life while you paid for it with the tax money they spent.

NESARA was supposed to be released to America on 9/11 because Bill Clinton, late in his last term in September 2000, was forced to sign the agreements to release a Gold-Backed Currency along with all the CIA evidence of the JFK murders and their crimes against humanity. The White Hats could not imagine that the Cabal would be that evil to destroy WTC One and Two, who housed the computers to run NESARA and the gold to finance it, and murder three thousand people, not to mention the countless thousands over the years as they trotted across the globe killing other innocents. In Building Seven, the CIA had hidden the documentation of their historical sickness, including Operation Mockingbird, to subterfuge a media that informed the people.

This lesson taught the Anti-Cabal of disregarding human life and their own need to re-sustain themselves with new funds knew no bounds. No longer can one party, the Democrats, be known as the evil group. Both ideological sides had to be destroyed by the Anti-Cabal in the Red Pill event.

5

THE GOLD STANDARD

Before we fully dive into the future nature of the Red Pill in the NESARA era, we need to drop back in time. *How to Return to the Gold Standard: The Major Obstacle to Monetary Reform is Ideological* by Bettina Bien Greaves (7) was a foundational conversation of an economist on how we could fix the Fed with a gold-backed currency all the way back in 1995.

Ms. Greaves was far ahead of her time concerning the Gold Standard for our money. But the Gold Standard was enacted in 1792 under the "Coinage Act" that established the US Mint and fixed the dollar upon a set of values as it interacted with gold. Only in 1862 (how fascinating that the Civil War brought about a financial departure from the Gold Standard) was the Legal Tender Act made to debut in the hearts and minds of the people translating paper money into currency. The Standard of Gold wasn't abandoned yet, but the writing was on the wall to create a Fiat currency that the Cabal would control.

Ms. Greaves indicated a few massive changes that would have to adjust the economic cognition to do the gold currency work: Firstly, it would have to balance the Federal Reserve's

Budget; secondly, stop inflation and Lastly, to stop welfare programs as a governmental entitlement. While each of these is debatable (Welfare chief among them), the first two focus upon the discussion.

The Federal Reserve has never let Congress peak at their Profit and Loss Statements or their Balance Sheet. The Fed is known as *the debt carrier of last resort* which means that when the economy is flailing as it did in the Great Depression and the Great Recession, it had to take the bad debts of the nation so that the Fiat would survive. Those toxic Fed debts could later be sold to another institution, most likely one of their banking buddies, at a significant profit, I might add.

To confirm the balancing of a budget, one must have a budget with which to operate. Think of a young couple fresh out of college as they start their dreams together. They haven't really been excellent in setting up their funds together, so they tragically spend like their incomes can manage the load. If she, God forbid, wishes to step away from the rigors of full-time employment raising the kids in those formative years, she cannot do so. That strain continues until both fight endlessly and seek financial restitution in Bankruptcy and later, a divorce. It's an all too familiar story. But to balance the Fed's budget would mean you would have to know it.

To stop inflation would strip the Fed's ability to increase the money flow, thereby the debt load upon the economy so that they can make some more dough! Inflation is a warm blanket around the financial gurus of today who can't imagine its death. But perish it will. We will peel off one of the axioms of faith in America: "the only two things you can trust is death and taxes." Income taxation is based upon inflation that creates a higher number each year to bloat the potential budget of the Cabal. They are playing cousins in the sandbox of the American economy.

Bettina also indicated that gold would "rise from $1705 an ounce to $7500 or more." Realize that gold in 1995 was only approximately $385 an ounce. In 2021, Gold has fluctuated wildly and was suppressed at 1700-1800 an ounce depending upon the fake market conditions. Ms. Greaves was using her almanac of the future to glean that prediction. But she indicated that the government should be prevented from interfering with the price of gold once the standard was set for the asset-backed currency. She opined that no one would care about the amount of the actual dollar instead of the purchasing power it would bring.

Value of Money vs. Pricing

Here, we can step forward several paces after the Red Pill and clue you into the ruminations of my mind. Today, in a Fiat currency, the value of plastic (debt/credit cards) is more important than the value of the money. You can leverage debt to further your position in all things, including buying houses then flipping them. If you do it correctly, whether by personal or corporate financials, increasing one's debt allows the ship's driver to gain position. You can take a flagging business; the build-up is the ability to make money upon its service, then you can sell it for a pretty penny. You never used your cash position to reduce the flow of your current needs. This is the power of using plastic to enrich your financial position in a Debt-Based economy such as the Fiat of the Fed affords intelligent people who understand it.

But when the value of the money becomes the virtual king, one must balance the potential risk that owning that asset might have. Could you make better money by holding that asset longer-term vs. the short-term gain by flipping that asset for more money? There will be a pregnant pause in economical thinking in the old ways of the Fiat. When cash is king, you will not choose to spend unwisely and be more careful about one's needs and wishes vs. the item's value.

The purchasing power of businesses and individuals will increase dramatically while prices decrease with a Gold/Asset economy. If the value is higher with the money, the prices will fall dramatically, as one values can do more for the value you have. Whereas, in a Fiat economy, the value of the money is significantly reduced as inflation rises.

The illegitimate and moronic Cabal member of Joe Biden rent the national structure nearly in two during his fraudulent term. Primarily, spending was out of control over Congress, White House, and Senate that had no dollar to their name. They were defunded by the Anti-Cabal due to their criminal actions with child trafficking, money laundering and drug schemes to steal from the world's people. During Biden's not too brief and false reign upon the Corporation of the defunct USA, prices rose dramatically as the cash value fell to record lows. Debt was incessantly high, meaning that there was no end in sight to the currency's value. Only in Germany after the Great mentioned above war in 1914-1918, we did also see the value of the currency drop to these insane levels. But that's all done and gone, isn't it? The Corporation is dead, and the Fiat with it. Somewhere in the background, I hear the high-pitched vocalizations, "the wicked witch is dead."

When a new economy emerges after the Red Pill, prices will fall as a brilliant comedic actor spills his body to play to the audience in slapstick. Some mistakenly believe that prices will drop to the 1950's of which I roll my eyes. Consider the nature of a house in the 1950s. It had so little of the electrical amenities that today's home has, not to mention the large sizes of the American homes of today. The ratios will be significantly lower but not be at 1950s pricing. But you won't care! You will never be able to imagine the buying power that your new gold-backed dollar affords you!

Other Potentials Imagined in 1995

Bettina also foresaw that the government would have to be out of the regulation of the Gold pricing. They would not be able to manipulate it as they have in 2020 and 2021. But she understood that the value of gold, unregulated, would stabilize once it would be tied to the currency. This makes utter sense.

The manipulation of currency was one of my questions when I studied the nature of the first crypto called Bitcoin at my mentor, Will. He wanted me to look into the tech of Bitcoin. When I thought that the currency could be placed upon Bitcoin for the new gold economy, he retorted that it could not.

"Why?" I asked.

"Blockchain was the brilliant structure of the Crypto. Bitcoin was created by the CIA and manipulated Cabal," Will answered.

It took me a few years to verify this point, but he was dead on. Blockchain tech could take a book to write its potential uses and is far above my head. What I will state about it is the simplicity of the tracking mechanism of the currency. If I give you ten bucks, then you take five to pay for coffee, the tracking of those three levels of purchase is done by the Blockchain tech. It is supposedly unhackable!

It has long been rumored that President Trump had the tech placed within the ballots to track what the accurate data was from the paper votes were. When the Cabal copied the ballots fraudulently, it was as easy as finding the difference between our current currency and Monopoly script in your wallet.

Ms. Greaves envisioned that the Government would be divorced from the monetary system. That's precisely what has to occur inside NESARA, where you kill off the Fed and unhook it from those who could manipulate it. She furthered reasoned the following probable scenarios:

1. No need for the FDIC (insurance for funds)
2. No Runs on the Bank.
3. No Fractional Banking creates a manipulated level of a new relationship with inflation.

The banks would be required to keep on hand the total value of the money deposited minus the loans that they have outstanding, showing their balance sheets to those regulators who may know the liquidity of the bank. If the funds were matched in the balance sheet, then a run on the banks for cash or Federally Insured funds by the Fed would not be needed for an economic crash. Most, if not all, economic downtrends were carefully created to steal from the people by the Cabal, so the above would not be needed to have a policing agency that is fraudulent on their own.

6

NESARA INGREDIENTS

Let's take a little bit to explain some of the inclusions to NESARA. Lots of people will give you so many other details that are extraneous that it's hard to focus upon them. But let's focus on a few of the elements within the NESARA plan. We will not talk about the gold currency because that's already been discussed since the value of your money will rise steeply.

IRS Cancellation

For years I would read of the Flat Tax group messages. They wished to cancel the graduated tax program of the Internal Revenue Service, and replace it with a 10% or 15% taxation to all parties. The calculation of the current tax protocol is so convoluted that you must use an accountant or have software to walk you through the maze of questions. If you own a business such as I do, there's no way you can get away without an accountant conversant upon the nuances of that tax code.

IRS taxation of people is clearly not constitutional and cannot be supported by anything other than fraudulent courts in a court of law. The reality is that the Income Taxation will be eliminated entirely. The IRS may play a small role in collecting a Federal Sales Tax, but I would suggest that they change the name and the staff of the existing agency.

Having a Federal Sales Tax of 14% would pay for all the needs of a federal government. It would include only new items but delete food and medicines. Therefore, if you bought a new car, you would have your city, state, and county tax along with a federal tax. But people complain about another tax since they hate taxation. But the beauty of a Federal Sales Tax is that it's really a Use Tax.

Who pays more in sales tax if one person makes $50,000 and another makes $150K? You got it. Big companies who buy a lot will pay more in only fair taxation, and it actually works.

Debt Jubilee

Easily one of the most controversial concepts is the Debt Jubilee. All money transfers (from bank to pay your credit card for the monthly draft) are a conduit within the Fed. How? Your Routing Number is a designator to the Fed to indicate the bank and location of that bank. This is called a SWIFT code in other circles of communication. The SWIFT system of money transfer is one of the most hackable sources of an individual.

Therefore, all banking and payments have some element of the SWIFT and Fed involvement when they occur. In October 2021, severe fervor existed over Biden's inclusion of any transfer of funds from any bank account over six hundred dollars reported directly to the IRS, and I found it laughable. ALL transfers are imminently viewable by the Cabal through the Fed!

After the typical endless paperwork that I have done so many times I can do them in my sleep, I was worried that I hadn't received the payment slip or even the company that purchased my loan. But in May of 2020, my friend and mortgage broker contacted me to say that rates were favorable for me to refinance my house and save about $140 a month. Before the loan company accomplished the final loan value in that interim phase, I was mailed the strangest letter I had ever opened.

The letter explained that Fannie Mae had purchased my loan. I was not to write them the monthly payments for my loan but to wait for the mortgage company. If you don't know who Fannie Mae is, this is one of the firms in the 2008 mortgage crisis that caused the Great Recession that was funding poor loans to people with poor credit that nearly crashed the entire economy. As a last resort for bad debts of horrendous portions, the Fed had taken over Fannie Mae and Freddie Mac.

Therefore, my loan is held in the Federal Reserve, as are all loans, either Business to Business or Personal to Business. When bankruptcy occurs on a corporate or private level, those loans are deemed uncollectable. Typically, the bank repossesses reusable property for secured loans such as cars and houses. But when the bank and the Fed have been deemed the frauds, who owns that property? You do! There is no one to repossess that property, because the banks were tied into the system and have committed the fraudulent and criminal enterprises that make up the stealing that had nearly sunk our nation. They are the reason that we have the debt. They criminally claim that we own the debt that they created.

To say it in another fashion, it would be similar to me buying a property with my next-door neighbor's credit report. Even though I possess that property, all the payments are from my neighbors. When I default on it, the property default and all interest payments are my neighbor's problem and not mine. Does that sound in the least fair? That's what the Fed, the Bankers, the Congress, and all the other Cabal members have done to you and me. They will receive NONE of the blessings of the debt forgiveness that comes.

Student loans, mortgage payments, car loans (includes leases), and credit cards will be paid off through your credit report. That's why the Anti-Cabal brought in the money to America that Obama blocked in The Hague court that I believe occurred back in 2009. That $87 trillion pays off the debts of the Fed and all our loans. The only loan that is not paid back is similar to my parents giving me money for the business, a person-to-person loan, and no bank can pay that back.

Since the Quantum Financial System (QFS) was potentially turned on in August 2020, it has been running in the background alongside the SWIFT system assessing the waters. It's two servers moving in concert with one another.

Many have personally reported the wiping of their debts in totality. That's the QFS testing the credit reports and intimating a change to kill off the loans. That person was not asked to return the property. That's coming, depending upon the moment that you read this book.

Constitutional Reform of the Courts

One of the biggest problems in the world is to note how unconstitutional our court systems are. The lawyers manipulate the system by emotion and subterfuge, and the judges find technicalities to delete real crimes and punish non-criminals by their whims.

If you hadn't seen a Constitutional Republic before, how would you know it would work? When John Adams, one of our Founding Fathers, envisioned America without a King (he firstly wanted Washington to take the role as a king, but George wouldn't hear of it) with absolute power, there was significant resistance. But Adams chose to help put three forms of a government to balance the other.

The Executive Branch leads and signs laws that the Congress begins, while the Senate confirms those laws. If Congress is wildly convinced by a proposition that the President vetoes, it can push the bill through without his/her consent with a two-thirds vote. Congress creates the bills that run the nation, including the money inside of a large pool of people to meet the Will of the People which is why they should be out of the office quicker. The Legal portion of the branches should oversee the Framer's original intent of the bills and check upon foreign and domestic activities of what the Executive Branch enacts.

But the court systems are badly fraudulent in their nature which has driven the ship of the country in the wrong direction ever since the founding of this corporation that mimics a Constitutional Government in almost any fashion. Did you know that the FBI believes that those who adhere to the principles of the Constitution are at odds with their democracy? I could use a cuss word here; what the ____?

Secondly, we are NOT a Democracy! Democracy was never what we were created to be. You must delete that from your dictionary. Democracy states that if the majority agrees with a position, it becomes the state's official code. That means that if 68% believe that being White is a crime against humanity, it can legislate their rights away irrespectively against the Constitutional mandates.

We are a Republic! That's a cadre of people living by a fundamental law that must be carefully amended (the Amendments) from time to time, if a position is out of balance from the Framer's original intent. Therefore, the Legislative Branch was meant to balance the Constitution and not the Democratic process! Even if Congress and the Senate strongly believe a course of action with a veto vote to overturn a bill, it can be struck down by the court system designed to protect the Constitution.

One of the most critical roles of NESARA is the deletion of the Corporation that the Cabal has set up. Once you delete the one thing corrupting the Constitution, you can return to America's founding principles. The American Bar Association (ABA) will be abolished in the new Republic, because its primary role is to maintain the Corporation.

NESARA means to retrain the judges and the lawyers to the original and only duty to the American people: to uphold the Constitutional values that are immutable for the people in justice. It doesn't mean that things are always fair. As I interviewed him for this book, I had a friend who didn't believe that lawyers would cease to exist in the NESARA era. Absolutely not!

In the Old Testament, God set up judges to rule over the people. The Father allowed the people to govern themselves inside of their loose territory, but when a situation arose that moved into a dispute, the judge would litigate the event with laws. That's how the judicial base was supposed to flow.

Some judges will be gone before NESARA is enacted in the Red Pill. One such is Chief Justice John Roberts of the Supreme Court. Roberts has been spotted in pictures and through signatures upon Epstein's Island, and the Lolita Express to the Island. Would this suggest that he is a massive pedo? Judge Roberts is also a part of stealing trillions of dollars of 9/11, which we discussed earlier.

Term Limits for Each Government Official

One reform necessary for the nation's health is to restore real term limits to governmental positions. It's interesting to note that one of my favorite (not anymore) presidents of the 20th century was FDR. He led the nation out of the Great Depression and successfully through a war-making America the unquestioned world power it would be for eighty years, until Joe Biden's incompetence. FDR ignored the term limits set by George Washington that were always known with two, four-year terms for Presidents.

I speculate that those limits will exist again for all branches of government. If they work through elected positions, a person can be elected to a Mayoral position then onto Congress, the US Senate, and maybe the Presidency. He or she would only be able to run for two terms per position which still is a relatively long time in public service.

The retirement plan that allows Federal service to receive 100% pension of their highest office will have to be immediately deleted, as these are either criminals or can create their own retirement plan just like everyone else in the private sector. Their health plan is beyond gawdy and must align with all other service branches. Once you delete the fat of the Lobbyists who wine and dine Senators to do their bidding and the above clauses, they have created for themselves, the budget is almost easy to maintain with a Federal Sales Tax revenue generation as well as Excise and Tariff taxes that the nation can receive to pay its way.

The Federal Government doesn't need Czars that existed in Obama's cabinet that dot the landscape of the swamp land of Washington,

DC. It should be limited to the House, Senate, Judicial, Executive, and Diplomatic services in a stripped-down fashion that allows the States to take primacy for the significant needs of the people. The Federal Government needs to have efficient investigative agencies after gutting the Cabal dotted their payroll. No more should authorities maintain control over the people without direct accountability over their actions.

There must be a healthy fear that their needs come first before the Senator's unimportant desires as she serves in office. She must be respectful and bound by those duties in a way that she has nothing but contempt with anything outside of that framework of demand. That's also why I believe that the two-party system must be abandoned, since they are both far too divisive and corrupt to remain.

I don't care if one candidate wants to fix the road system and the other wants to heal the public school system. If a person wins that position, select either one and let nothing get in her way of that job. The whole body must bring her into that office in pure elections that create unity for the time. Of course, there will be bitter disagreements, but they must be civil with the people in mind without the ridiculous stalling that one side does to the other before they campaign for re-election, doing nothing in the process of their term.

7

BIBLICAL IMPACT OF THE RED PILL

One of the biggest struggles with the topic of the Red Pill is the audacity of the idea. To intimate that your government and trusted sources have been lied to you about almost every concept in American history is too ludicrous for the mind to conceive. Even those who have already Red Pilled themselves years ago, we have been asking ourselves: how deep does the rabbit hole go?

Must we consider Aliens? How about a flat earth? What about JFK Junior being alive? It can be loony to conjure. But I choose to focus my energies on what I know from a Biblical perspective. Inside of the Word of God, we have an almost endless supply of verses that seem to be too gigantic for the task of placement within our world. One feature that is constantly missing from the Social Media drivel upon Biblical topics is taking what is eternal (the Word) and subjugating it within the temporal (our personal history of the now). But let's organize the Bible in a slightly unique way to analyze the verses I will contend.

The Israelites contain a significant portion of

God's heart that spans from the Old Testament into the first five books of the New Testament. Matthew, Mark, Luke, John and Acts hold separate accounts of the central character's life long-awaited in the Old Testament called the Messiah who would save the world. Jesus fulfills the role in numerous prophecies that contain His First Coming. His role as the Son of God and the executor of the Will of the Father finalizes humanity in the place, so that she can achieve, by belief in Jesus as her Savior, can save us from the laws of God that only explain that one must be perfect.

So many who read the Scriptures believe that the Law was meant to be prescriptively followed by humanity in Hebraic fashion to attain everlasting life. We read the book of Romans that Paul, the articulate Apostle who was a prescriptive Jew inside the Sanhedrin who was humbled to become the greatest purveyor of the completeness of Jesus, told that the Law was to describe man's relationship to sin. Paul later purports that it was utterly hopeless to achieve that perfection inside the Law. Paul indicated that Jesus was the "source and perfector of our faith, who for the joy that lay before Him endured a cross and despised the shame and has sat down at the right hand of God's throne (Hebrews 12:2 HCSB)."

The second phase of Scriptural understanding is the nature of the Bride of Christ which is the Church. The books mentioned above that Paul and others indicate to understand what the believer has given upon the world to follow a higher calling of Christ.

This culminates in the Second Coming of Christ.

Those verses dot the Old and New Testament, since they include the Remnant of God which are the Jews coming back into the bosom of the Father in the Millennial Reign of Christ where Jesus returns to rule from Jerusalem. Approximately one thousand verses detail the seven-year Tribulation and the Millennial Reign (one thousand years) journey for humanity.

We finalize our existence in the destruction of the universe through fire that comes just after the verdict of the wicked dead called the White Throne Judgment. After that, all of humanity who was redeemed by the blood of Jesus for what their faith told them to believe will live an eternity with God the Father, Son and Holy Spirit in a new heaven and earth. I have studied Eschatology for more than thirty-six years to understand what the future holds for us. I have also found that we need to understand the First Coming before adequately dealing with the Second Coming.

Now that I overviewed the Bible for you in a shortened theological study, I need to move you to verses that indicate an interim timeframe in the Church Age (which begins at Jesus' death and ends at the beginning of the Tribulation in Revelation 6). Some verses make no sense to the nature of either reality that I tended, until 2020, to put aside.

Corruption Enters my Life to Kill me

End Time verses are notable in that they

come to the placement of Jesus beginning the Tribulation by introducing the Anti-Christ upon the scene (Revelation 6) all the way until He steps upon the planet to begin the Millennial Reign. It takes a long time to see their organization, and that's why Prophecy Teachers exist. But I must digress into the path that led me to the place of this book and my Social Media conjectures on Facebook (through the myriad bannings of idiot Fact Checkers), Twitter, YouTube and Telegram channels of the Conspiracy theories.

In December of 2019, I took my family to Denver, watching the Colorado Avalanche get beaten in the third period by the Chicago Blackhawks. My wife and I decided to celebrate my son's 21st birthday in the city of his birth and my childhood by indulging in a fascination that had burgeoned that year of the National Hockey League with his father. But the morning of December 22, I awoke in the hotel, telling them I was not feeling well. Within twenty minutes, it was all that the two of them could do to load me into the car to speed to the nearest hospital.

Within minutes of arriving, I was presenting with a severe stroke, and my wife was being told to fear the worst. The ER Physicians were sure I could either die or be permanently injured. The MRI would clearly reveal the neurological damage showing psychosis and an inability to communicate clearly. But, the MRI was clean. The Physicians pivoted to assure my wife, a Master's prepared R.N. herself, regarding the new diagnosis of Encephalopathy that the CT

Scan would indeed reveal. When that was being scheduled shortly, my reasoning had disappeared, and my psychosis was presenting with terrifying rapidity. A lumbar puncture was needed to determine the exact nature of my illness, on top of the CT Scan.

By the time I was moved to the ICU for critical care, the CT had returned negative, and the lumbar puncture didn't find any neurological viruses or bacterial infections in the spinal column. My psychosis could not be controlled, and I was posey restrained to the bed. During that Sunday (December 22), I only had visions of a spirit realm about me. There were four demons that I finally realized (only months later, after much consideration) were fighting a battle against four angels about my bed frame. I screamed in the middle of the fight over which I had no control.

My ministry partner, Sue Reidel, was praying from Tulsa over my spirit all that night. She saw a verse brought to my bed by those four angels as a blanket that covered me inside Psalms 91. Psalms 91 has several famous quoted verses that have been used inside of World War One for both sides of the trench warfare when they crawled to battle their foe "though a thousand fall at your side and ten thousand at your right hand, the pestilence will not reach you (vs. 7)." Sue relied upon that verse for healing over me with the battle she was correctly sensing that I was in the middle of. But she didn't understand the gravity of the following verse I still hold onto daily.

"You will only see it with your eyes and

witness the punishment of the wicked" is spoken by David in verse eight (for the rest of this story, you can go to my book on DrScottYoung.com "Near Diagnosis Experience"). So, few ever quote this verse that it's hard to understand the placement in the history of the verse. This verse seems to be an End Time verse on the surface but cannot be due to its written.

"You will only see it with your eyes..." indicates that one must be in person with his/her physical eyes to note the punishment of wicked people. If you read earlier, I mentioned the End Times. People center upon two sections of massive punishment of wickedness for our future.

One is in Revelation 14:17-19, where the Angels are stomping the grapes into the winepress of the wrath of the Lamb. This refers to a moment at the end of the Tribulation where Jesus steps upon the planet to finalize His wrath. If you believe in a Post-Tribulation Rapture of the Church (meaning that the Church leaves at the last possible moment which is now referred to as the Pre-Wrath Position), then we as the Bride of Christ should already be gone. If, on the other hand, you believe in the Pre-Tribulation Rapture of the Church, which is the position that we leave the planet in the Rapture before the Tribulation, then we would obviously be long gone before the inclusion of this verse.

Psalms 91:8 directly stipulated that "you will only see with your eyes and witness..." meaning that we must be in the flesh to see it. You cannot be seeing this in the spirit. If that is true, I passionately believe and teach that all Scripture is true (read II Timothy 3:16), then we must conclude that this is one of those strange verses that have nothing to do with the End Times.

With that backdrop of a verse that has been undeniably unquenched throughout the history of a mass level of punishment by humanity of the wicked in physical form, we come to the conclusion that this verse has not happened yet. But, it also won't be an End Time verse for the reasons above. It must occur before the Tribulation.

James 5:3-7

Your silver and gold are corroded, and their corrosion will be a witness against you and will eat your flesh like fire. You stored up treasure in the last days! Look! The pay that you withheld from the workers who reaped your fields cries out, and the outcry of the harvesters has reached the ears of the Lord of Hosts. You have lived luxuriously on the land and have indulged yourselves. You have fattened your hearts for the day of the slaughter. You have condemned – you have murdered – the righteous man; he does not resist you. Therefore, brothers, be patient until the Lord's coming. See how the farmer waits for the precious fruit of the earth and is patient with it until it receives the early and late rains.

I could spend hours upon the nature of these beautifully terrible verses. Firstly, one's silver and gold are corroded, indicating that those corrupted have received it criminally by the wicked's actions. Their crimes become cries against them and a protest to God. Huh...well, that sounds like the Cabal to me. These verses are definitely not talking ONLY about the end. They reference the end in a few ways, but there's a deeper resonance about the context of the verses regarding holy payback or retribution.

These are murderers who haven't paid those of the harvesters. Through the Holy Spirit, James could have used workers of any type here: carpenters, craftsmen, or other laborers, and he uses explicitly a farming reference. If you remember earlier in the book, we identify that NESARA comes from the work of Farmers against those inside of the Federal Reserve (or called the Farm Bureau). Why would the Bible bring a particular group of workers to the forefront haphazardly to reference them to the corruption along with silver and gold references? I believe it's another Biblical code that relates to our timeframe.

The Holy Spirit never obfuscates the wording He carefully crafts through the human writers. When the verses indicate they are a witness, it is the Greek word for *Martyrion* that means that if one presents evidence in court that is false, she may have to pay the penalty of death for her crimes. That's how the Bible and ancient times considered lying under oath. The wickedness of the Cabal will be seen in the courtroom and be found as their evidence in the final execution of Tribunal Justice.

Debt Jubilee in the Old Testament

"You are to consecrate the fiftieth year and proclaim freedom in the land for all its inhabitants. It will be your Jubilee, when each of you is to return to his property and each of you to his clan (Leviticus 25:10 HCSB)." This is the purpose of the Debt Forgiveness of which I believe is coming. It intimates the property coming back to the person in his own land. It doesn't only mean your house, but it also refers to your possessions. It must come from those who have tried to take it. The government will have to give it back. The people of ancient times didn't like this practice. When they didn't do it, God made them complete the Jubilee by allowing them to be enslaved, so that the people could get it back.

Job 27:17

"He may heap it up, but the righteous will wear it, and the innocent will divide up his silver." Man, this one excites me! In the Book of Job, our main character conversed with his evil friends more than the much wiser but younger friend who challenges him back at the very end of the book. God hears Job's complaints but tells him that He is the God above all the earth. This portion of the Word is the beginning of wisdom in investigating the question of evil.

But this verse cannot be an End Time event. Why? In the Tribulation, for the whole planet, everything gets worse, including those with any level of wealth. No one is exempt from the levels of judgment that come. The purpose of the Tribulation is to wake the world up from their ignorance of God.

One of the first prophetic events in the path of Eschatology is the Ezekiel 38-39 War. Here Russia and many of her Muslim brothers will conspire against Israel to come down upon their lands in the eastern mountains to carve out the territory of the Jews. But God reigns down a confusion weapon similar to the singers in the front line spoken of in II Chronicles 20, where the enemy kills one another in a judgment against themselves. After they kill one another in those eastern mountains, they experience a localized earthquake and then lastly, a tactical nuclear strike that irradiates the land for seven months until the Jews can bury them. It is foretold that the Israelites can take their fuel from the burnt wreck of the armies over the next seven years for their needs. This limited war is one of the most significant indicators that this has not happened yet and that it is Pre-Tribulational, meaning that it occurs before the Tribulation.

During the Tribulation, the people will not be obtaining more wealth, but only procuring the base means, as they suffer under the wrath of the Anti-Christ upon the world "Woe to you people of the earth for the devil has come down with great wrath knowing that his time is short (Revelation 12:7 HCSB)." The above Job verse is in stark contrast to the End Time verses, because the people listed in this verse will be taking up the spoils that the wicked people were storing for themselves. "The righteous will wear it" also informs the reader that it's more than mortgage property but is what one might wear such as jewelry or clothes that are expensive. The wicked will be left with nothing.

Psalms 37:21

"The wicked man borrows and does not repay, but the righteous one is gracious and giving." So utterly fascinating. Some use this verse as a sword over the borrower (the one who needs to pay). That would be unwise to apply it as such. Too many Cabalists, including Nancy Pelosi, take money from the government (your tax money from the IRS that doesn't pay for anything to run the government) to buy properties. They never pay it back. How can so many professional services have so many billions to spend like their Cabalist billionaire friends. They bilk so the people, complete insider trading (while punishing others for their own crimes), and use their purchasing power without ever giving it back. This is one significant definition of wickedness.

But when the Red Pill occurs, there's a rude awakening for the Cabal. Their families will receive nothing! They will be penniless, at best, if they have only taken money or looked the other way from the wickedness. If they have done worse, such as the child trafficking and the killing of innocents along with the stealing of most people's fortunes, they will pay with their lives.

STAGES OF GRIEF AFTER THE RED PILL

"How can I have been lied to for my entire life?"

"Why didn't I know about the corruption, but you did?"

"It can't be as bad as I am hearing. Maybe some of this is false?"

These are but a few of the questions or comments that you will hear. They are exactly what you felt some months or years ago, as you came into the truth of the Cabal and their nefarious activities. Their nature is so evil that the Bible uses the wording called wicked. I believe that those who are wicked have long ago made a choice against God, knowingly, to follow the path of Satan. They clearly see the option and have made it. The situation with the Tribunals and subsequent totality of executions on a mass scale will align with Old Testament ideals, in which the people needed to be eradicated. They have chosen against any level of redemption. Don't ask me for mercy.

How can there be No Redemption for these Wicked People of the Cabal?

I have spent years upon this topic and bantered it with my wife who has her master's in Psychiatric Nursing. Portions of my spirit react to those closest to me, be they employees or friends, who extend a significant grace to them through their faults, sometimes to the irritation of my wife who was long done with the person's destructive behaviors. On the other hand, my wife has a tender spirit against people we don't know. I tend to lean toward a harsher level of judgment on those who have made sick choices all their lives. But one thing we both agree: harming of a child, and there is no reduced sentence in our books.

At the first Freedom Conference put on by Clay Clark, a quirky host that moves the meeting along efficiently, the spirit of mostly Christians was grace-filled. There were tender moments of grace to those who just didn't know about COVID and those effects upon their bodies. But as soon as Jim Caviezel spoke upon his movie called "The Sound of Freedom" which was released in 2023 began to speak along with his research colleague upon the nature of Child Trafficking, the mood quickly turned sullen with the two thousand people at Rhema Church in Broken Arrow, Oklahoma.

Jim intoned: "No Mercy" about those who have imprisoned, raped and killed children for years. Not one person in the room disagreed; that's the Cabal's Achilles Heel. They have used children for their sick games of extracting

Adrenochrome and sexual pleasures for many years until the child is used up. They then choose to murder the child when he or she is not worth the effort.

The first time I killed an animal hunting as a child, it took a toll on my spirit even though I had been taught to respect the animals. My father was careful to utilize all the meat of the deer and not let it suffer. Those who have studied the path of mass murderers know that those sociopaths move from harming animals for their sick pleasures to deepening levels of torture, until they practice it upon humans. Once they do it upon an adult, they rarely move downward to children. God forbid the inmate before the Red Pill to be known in general population for child molestation; he won't last long. It's even that deplorable for the hardened criminals within their code of ethical violations.

Then consider the path of the Cabal. One might enter Congress seeking to do good. But once he senses the money and the women that come his way, the Cabal prods the individual's psyche to find his weaknesses. The Playboy Mansion with Hugh Hefner was the sixties and seventies version of the Cabal's attempt to find those weaknesses fully endorsed and funded by the CIA. If that Congressperson stops at the level of the cash bribes and the compromising positions with various women to the detriment of his personal life, then they have that guy for his whole career. If he doesn't toe the line that the Cabal's train is heading, he is constantly threatened by revealing his indiscretions. Many of those people have fallen over the years for those reasons once they rocked the boat deeply enough to tick off their handlers.

When one considers the more profound nature of the drivers of the Cabal, the rabbit hole takes turns that you can scarcely imagine. If the person is a noted sociopath, such as Nancy Pelosi or her nephew Gavin Newsome who has some intelligence but no personal inner sanctum of conscience, the depth of the disease sinks to taking a child and a gun. Firstly, they are told to rape the child and kill her while it's recorded for ammo against non-compliance. Epstein Island and others just like it worldwide are systemic cancers of the soul that need to be cut out, burned to the ground, and destroyed all those who participate in the brutalization of tens of thousands of innocents yearly. You cannot allow them to exist upon the planet. As a society with laws, you must send them to their chosen maker, Satan, for the reality of their crime. Hell will not be a pleasant place for these sickos.

You will be shocked to find out those pretty faces on TV, and the Silver Screen with perfect jowl lines are the worst in a spiritual sense. They have spent a life pushing down those underneath them with frightening rapidity. I have spent enough time around the celebrity mentality personally to know that unless you are deemed worthy of being in their presence, you are far below their station to the level of a servant or a slave. This is when you know you have reached the depth of contempt for humanity that must be cut out for our societal norms to return to sanity.

Stages of That Grief of Lies

When my wife lost her mom to vascular dementia (loss of brain function due to poor blood flow), Wendy walked through the Stages of Grief, which she taught for many years beforehand. They are the following:

Denial – This minimizes the overwhelming pain of the loss. The new reality of the situation doesn't override what the person wishes; therefore, they experience a Cognitive Dissonance (separating from what is believed vs. what is real).

Anger – The problem of the new reality creates anger that is not easily quelled by logic or reason. One must deal with their anger of the loss.

Bargaining – Once the person enters this phase, they seek outside counsel and including God to reconcile the grief. Here the person pushes external forces to return to the old stage of existence.

Depression – When depression sets in, no one can reason enough with the person. She must live this loss for a time, meaning that eating and sleeping are seriously disrupted until that loss is grasped.

Acceptance – At the end of the psychological journey of the Stages of Grief, the person begins to accept the new reality as the primary one and seems to move on.

The misnomer about the Stages of Grief is that you progress through those stages linearly, so that each can be processed emotionally, mentally, and willfully as the soul advances to the next supposedly logical phase. But it doesn't work that way. You will slide in and out of these phases, and possibly skip a stage. Instead of a straight line, a young child's scribbled drawings of what she sees are more likely the grief path.

The different reality is that grief isn't set inside of the loss of a person through death but can be felt for job losses, relationship breakups and many other personal factors. Some people almost live inside the phases in an endless loop of grief never to emerge. Wendy and I had an employee that spent her five-year tenure with us constantly battling her grief until it was her companion. Any level of change, including replacing an old printer and a secondary scanner that took up extra desk space, was met with tears of loss. These people have hijacked their grief for so long that they have poisoned their souls to not be able to hear the truth when it comes to their doorstep.

The Red Pill upon the Population

When I was a teenager, I sickly marveled at my grandmother (a Greatest Generation person) who screamed at her Soap Operas for the woman to flee from the fictional menace of the antagonist man. The first time she did it, I searched the room for the threat level she displayed with her verbal tone. Once I understood that her terror was directed at the program, I uttered loud enough, "Gramma! They aren't real!"

Many people will come to a poor reality that their heroes in the media, social media, Hollywood and Government were all frauds and Satanists killing kids for their pleasure. They must witness the crime recorded clearly showing the nature of the wickedness; a massive level of Cognitive Dissonance will exist for quite some time.

Most people who watch the modern horror flicks (I cannot even watch the trailers) have purveyed the wickedness of people who harm others in grotesque fashions. It's interesting to note that video games in which your Role Playing Game (RPG) character who rids his existence of evil people see only masked or alien creatures with whom they can kill. It's not the pretty people who are murdered in the games, because game-makers who long know that too much reality would not sell their game.

The producers portray those in horror flicks are portrayed as sickos by the producers until we reach films like "Silence of the Lambs." In that film, we note a character who is a Physician who was intelligent and well-mannered behind a glass prison for his horrific crimes of eating people that he killed for his sadistic pleasure that might have had a sexual element to the crime. These movies take it to the next level when we cannot quickly identify those bad guys in the older Horror Films of "Freddie's Nightmare." Grotesque figures are so much easier to revile.

When the people of the planet find out how disgusting their leaders and heroes are, shock isn't even the correct term to describe what might occur. In the next chapter, I would like to detail what I think is for the world. You will feel it as well (to a lesser degree depending on how long it has been since you have been Awakened) learning about those you may have admired in the past. The Red Pill Psychological effects will be felt for years, until the Tribulation in which Jesus begins to break down the rest of the world for the Millennial Reign of Christ.

9

PSYCHOLOGICAL IMPACT OF THE RED PILL

I have puzzled over the Red Pill for some time. Firstly, I conceived of a moment in which I would jump to the ceiling (I used to have a 33" vertical leap playing basketball in my youth that is now down to five inches with knee injuries). For me, it's a celebration of what I have researched to know that I could be vindicated. Many Patriots feel the exact way. But I propose we consider those who will find this time quite the opposite.

Potential Phases of Impact

1. Fear and Anxiety

You will find concepts that you might have experienced through your own Stages of Grief process, but these are modified by the witty help of Wendy Young, my brilliant wife!

When fear and anxiety come together, they are a lethal cocktail inside all citizens. Fear and anxiety can increase blood pressure and heart rate. Fear is the momentary reaction of danger to oneself, whether psychological or physical peril. It's a natural and effective reaction to the transitory happenings we find ourselves within. If a potential attacker stalks up from behind in a darkened parking lot, your senses might run through a series of Fight or Flight physiological triggers. To fight is to eliminate the threat with your physical force to remove that attacker's ability to harm you. Your body needs that extra adrenaline boost to move away from the pending jeopardy to react in the flight. Some researchers actually have postulated, in recent times with the obeyance of one's smart phone in the hand of the prey, that a blinding effect can also occur. The target of the aggressor pauses, as if there is an internet buffering taking place inside of the body, freezing his motion. It's perfect for the assailant to experience his prey upon that moment of fear. They are easy.

Anxiety only comes in humans when we constantly reinforce that potentially harmful to our psyche or body. It may logically occur for those people who live in danger daily with abusive family members or an abusive boss in the workplace. It creates a physical barrier with which to allow the prey to cope with her environment daily.

When you multiply people's beliefs into a miasma of doubt within the Red Pill, the fear and anxiety will manifest in ways that only arise when societies break down during the war. A few films have captured this type of normative understanding better than the 1984 version of "Red Dawn." The Soviets, along with their Central American allies, invade from south of the border and deep into Colorado. The story highlights teenagers who have lost their families and futures. They learn to fight for a concept of America that had been lost. Freedom becomes a thing of the past (by the way, that does sound somewhat familiar inside the fake Biden Administration). It's well worth the watch.

Those who have not been Red Pilled before the global event that comes with the Media and Social Media takedown of the lies blocking so many truths from surfacing will suddenly not go to work. They will become severely impulsive to purchase goods in mass quantities, as if the world were ending. In their minds, it has.

In the first phases of Grief, the people will find little comfort with friends and family struggling with the same loss flipping what was believed as truth as impotent lies portrayed by the fake media who cannot support them by their platform. These individuals may resort to suicide and mass homicide. This is why we would need the military to institute some level of Marshall Law with a significant presence around all cities and towns. Note that Trump is the only President in recent history who had not introduced a new war to America. That was on purpose. Those military and authority agencies such as the Sheriffs, our real line of defense against completely corrupt political hacks who hate their nation, will step in to right the ship. But the turbulence will not be slight.

2. Disbelief and Anger

It is my opinion that the world will, even after hearing indisputable truth, not believe it. How can I even claim indisputable? Knowing that they need to prove their case on many levels, the White Hats will have video feeds of the severe misdeeds of the Cabal and confessions of their crimes along with documentation to prove beyond a reasonable doubt that the crime was committed. Military Tribunals are on the obfuscations that the current corrupt court system ignores the rules of law in the world, including foundational principles such as the Constitution. Nope, the Tribunals will require the liars to present their crimes in stunning detail.

You must realize something I have been studying for years now: these liars of the Cabal believe that they are constant winners and above the law. They believe their misdeeds are trivial in the global scheme of the process of ridding the world of Freedom. They think you need the structure only an ascended being, such as themselves, can bring by an Iron Fist rule. The Cabal wishes you would *just submit;* it is their battle cry. They genuinely don't comprehend why the people won't commit to them. They conjure, cajole, and use false logic based upon their own authority as truth givers. During Veteran's Day in 2021, CNN thanked the troops of present and past for their service. But they pridefully added their role as digital soldiers of the truth and that they needed a day to recognize their contribution to our Democracy. Crazy, huh?

In the face of that type of indoctrination of the public based upon the MK Ultra Program employed by the CIA through the Media and Hollywood freaks, they have leveled truth as a moving target as it suits their needs. If truth changes based upon Democratic views (called Pragmatism), then they've got you where they want you. You cannot mentally wriggle out of their hold by opposite levels of logic presented by a precious few that they have deemed Conspiracy Theorists who are lunatics.

At the point of the Red Pill, when they have to entertain that stage of Cognitive Dissonance unparalleled in their lives, disbelief and doubt will prevail. These people in this Stage may lash out at others in crazy ways. Be prepared.

In Denver, after my Broncos won their first Super Bowl in the 1997 season against Green Bay who was a 14-point favorite, I was ecstatic. I had never experienced a year like that as a long-time NFL fan of Denver. My best friend from high school, Eric Rognmoe, and I jumped and hugged, as John Elway kneeled in the victory formation that signaled the win. As Wendy and I drove home from the people who hosted the Super Bowl, a random car honked at Stop Sign. I looked about me to find the possible infraction I had just committed. There was none! The whole city was celebrating together something they had wished for since the team's founding more than thirty years prior. It occurred on every corner as we arrived home forty-five minutes later in thick Sunday traffic. Unfortunately, that night also held riots in downtown 16th Street Mall with idiots who turned over police cars not really celebrating but looking for the excuse to express pent-up emotions.

3. Regaining of Hope

An amazing transition will occur for the population after a few weeks to months of losing impulse control and immobilizing the world's people. Hopefully, there will be some like yourselves who were long Red Pilled, who are at the starting line of your life, ready to race when the Red Pill initiates. As they navigate their grief, you will see an ability to run ahead of your neighbors and friends. You will not have that same reaction. You will see NESARA popping up all around you and begin to operate within that freedom you have never really known.

We have discussed the nature of the Debt Jubilee that NESARA brings, but how it is perceived will be fascinating. If you knew all this was to occur, you would begin to think of your life in a new way. Later in this chapter, I will bring the quotation of Daniel who runs a Telegram blog called Silence Dogoode, MBA. When I discussed this book with him, he gave me some interesting tidbits that I will let you feast upon.

Among some of the ideas, others and I have discussed in the NESARA era outside of the releasing of debt are how the money changeover might feel to the individual who has been robbed for generations. She will sense a hope she has never experienced in the liberty that money can bring. Please don't misunderstand this: I am not talking about greed. That's the misplaced view of using wealth to empower oneself outside of the world's needs.

Money is only a vehicle. I don't care if you are

a believer in Christ and the Biblical principles therein, or you are a Patriot unsure of the Bible and Jesus. Both Patriots need to be thinking about how their own money solves themselves first, of course. They also then, once the reality of the money as it affords their life, to peer outward from the self to the benefit of your neighbors and those less fortunate themselves.

I personally do not ascribe to a UBI. The UBI is a Universal Basic Income that the Great Reset people, including Bernie Sanders, popularized over the past several years. It indicates that *all* people must be given an income such as $3000-5000 monthly as a payback from the Cabal for the wrongs that were done, not including the debt relief that they will experience when the Cabal banking dies. Some have seen the documentation of NESARA ascribing that people will receive millions of dollars per month for eleven years.

To have lottery-level wealth all at once creates a population that doesn't go to work would be disastrous. If no one has to work, we will have a bankruptcy in short order and economic crisis because the newly wealthy have received riches beyond their understanding. Google the ills that the sudden wealth of lottery winners do to people that come from little to millions all at once. They have no coping mechanism for that type of public wealth. Family and long ago acquaintances pop out of the woodwork to claim their own piece of the pie, guilting the person who sob stories and relationship strings to extract their portion of what they feel they deserve of the new millionaire. This would be multiplied on a scale hitherto unknown in human history. I frankly shutter to think of that dumping of money upon the entire population, no matter the arguments. It would be a population ruin of epic proportions.

Trump actually has claimed that his next term would have teemed with the opportunity to expand to one million new businesses created. I didn't say jobs; I said *businesses*! If a business employs dozens of workers per successful venture, you can see that this goal would mean dozens of millions of new and well-paying jobs. But people need to create the wealth without it being stolen by the Cabal, as it has in the past through income taxation and fractional banking. Listen to *Silence* talk about his vision below.

I believe the mission and vision of any business can expand outward to serve more customers in a post-NESARA era. Dreams can become realities. The time spent on bureaucratic red tape can go back into training, research and development, and rewarding employees with profit sharing. This will help the economy, as more people enjoy the fruits of their labor, borrow, spend and enjoy a healthier lifestyle with less stress.

Humans are very nimble and can adapt to change under new and unforeseen environments. They will go through the Five Stages of Grief but will come out on the other side strong and better prepared to serve new clients in the new era.

When income taxes cease, this will give the economy a sudden jolt. Things will balance out as some professionals may find their work meaningless or nonexistent in the NESARA era. Others will be inundated with work, while others again may see the writing on the wall that it's time to start a business.

The entrepreneurial spirit of America has slowly been sucked out of her, and it will gradually return. It will certainly return. The Millennials may very well be the last generation of corporate grifters, while the younger generation of kids under eighteen have watched everything in the world play out. Recent statistics put high schoolers wanting to go to a four-year college at under 50%, down from 72% pre-plandemic. That is a sudden and dramatic change that I think frankly woke colleges unprepared for and cannot see the difference that is about to hit them. Trade schools, non-woke, and community colleges are set to do very well in the years ahead.

The system's invisible hands now rely on the government bureaucracy to maintain enough of the status quo to keep people stuck in their 9-5 jobs. Healthcare benefits are one of the biggest (inhibitors) and 401K, Dental and Disability Insurance, and they offer a steady paycheck. As unappealing as some aspects of doing something you hate, the trade-off is not having to deal with the litany of complexities to go out on your own, so people suck it up and maintain that status quo. Not to mention, the educational system has failed us, so many people would be a lost puppy in a swamp to try to navigate the business world.

Most people are disconnected spiritually from the physical world that we only live in temporarily. If you study pricing throughout the history of America, there was deflation throughout the 1800s with only minor bouts of inflations that mainly occurred during the Civil War. There were periods of hyperinflation in the 1700s when different monetary systems experimented with. After creating the Fed in 1913, the third Central Bank since our nation's founding, the Cabal have intentionally made inflations and deflation cycles that create a massive boom or bust economy. I believe that the role of government should be limited, although I do think that they must protect the people from our enemies, foreign and domestic. I believe that the US Constitution under Section One, Article Ten grants the right of only the government to print money as legal tender.

The Fed is a shame, and we work under the confines of Admiralty Law with codes and rules, and the lands of the Federal Serve branches are legally considered foreign lands. In the new system of NESARA, all professionals will need to be re-tooled and retrained on the inner workers, which is where people like you and I will step in to teach. However, I believe the truth will be much easier for people to learn, but their souls will also connect deeper. The people will be aligned with things they want to do instead of things they are indirectly forced to do due to the lack of money or education. (Silence Dogood, MBA writing on November 12, 2021, directly to Scott and with his permission. Some excerpts were removed to create a word flow only. Silence also told me that it took him a few weeks to gather his thoughts, but the Lord gave him this prophecy).

10
HOW WILL NESARA MONEY CHANGE BUSINESS?

Once NESARA occurs only after the Red Pill initiates through the Emergency Broadcast Signal (EBS), we start to see the changes step up quickly. Of course, you had to wade through the lawsuits that will come against Physicians/Hospitals over the vax, as well as the industries that trade in the illegal imprisonments and raping of children. The court systems will be retrained, as Silence Dogood MBA predicts, and then they will have a backlog of cases that will be resolved in short succession.

When I had a patient who claimed that I didn't do him right and wanted to have his money returned for the hearing aids I did on him (complete silliness from the get-go and asked for *two years later*), I prayed that no one would view my company carried through the mud. I was dismayed to watch a filled courtroom when my case was heard after the summons. There were literally fifty cases in front of me. But most of them were dismissed out of hand until three cases were left (I won due to the illogic of the claim). Why? Because the defendants of the claim (foreclosure mostly) never showed up for the hearing. If you are taken to court, you lose if you don't show up, no matter how righteous your claim is! I believe that will be a portion of many cases against the Cabal and these sickos who have harmed the world. The evidence against their claims has been and will be established that anyone harmed will win "out of hand."

But as the dust clears over the next few months, businesses will start to consider a new reality. They will ask many questions I would like to pose and answer. Remember, I don't know all the potential variables, but we can surmise some of them.

How will Biz Redefine Ethics be considered in light of the Cabal's Evil?

This question may not be foremost in your mind to start with, and since there is no natural order of which to conjure first, I think it's pretty germane. Years ago, the state of OK decided to require Audiologists to have four hours of ethics to keep their licensure. They would not allow the course, unless they knew the complete details of the course before approving it (they were forcing us to go to their events). It was a joke, and all of us knew it.

How do you claim that you can address ethics in the light of no Moral Code? You can't. Ethics only come from a moral home plate. If you have a moral base, then ethics always follow from first base all the way home. They come in the form of a Policy/Procedure manual written by moral people! But when moral people are not deriving the basis of ethics, then we have a big problem.

Governments, Big Tech and big corporations have no ethical value constant within them, because we will see how little moral value they hold in killing and raping children, imprisoning the helpless, and stealing your money in nefarious ways. How can anyone listen to the nature of a governing body when it comes to ethics in the light of the necessary moral code lacking in the Cabal who have controlled our governments?

Once truly moral people find they have been lied to, they will begin to ask the critical questions that all of my Telegram channel asks me daily: prove it! If I don't verify a topic, I am called out on it, especially on my Social Media Channels. *Veritas* is one of the most beautiful words in Greek. It's where we derive one level of Truth. How do you know Truth if you can't verify it? You can't! Once you find that most authorities have lied to you, you will seek those with truth and query them! That's an outstanding level of knowledge that the teachers you surround yourself with are steeped in telling the truth through the verification process. Good science has been lost for far too long with a horrible and unverifiable lack of science such as Evolution and vaccine research, which must be reborn, as do best business practices.

I work with a consulting group called Audigy in Portland, Oregon. Even with all their faults, they endeavor to glean the Best Business Practices of the Audiology owners to create effective Policies and efficient procedures to run those businesses. They will need to be Red Pilled just as much as anyone else. But this will spur new growth in evaluating all the processes we consider ethical today.

How do hospitals recreate their image in the face of so much negativity along with the COVID and vaccine obvious failures? How will they punish those in charge (more likely, the White Hats will drag the policy makers from the Hospital systems to prison) to create new concepts in healthcare? How will they utilize tried and true Ivermectin and Hydroxychloroquine into their daily routines to treat cases of flu that kill many people yearly, outside of the COVID craziness?

How will businesses learn that ethics can lead you into great responses with your clientele? I believe that once small and medium-sized companies come to grips with the lies of the world, they will begin to rewrite policies. Which ones? The stances to require vaccinations of their employees! But ethics can only be defined inside of one's moral standards. Once those are clearly identified for the corporate leaders, the ethics will be revamped.

How will you Trust Businesses when the Lack of Trust is Revealed?

Consider a company like McDonald's. They have kept up with the leftist bull of woke politics. It's long been rumored that they have human flesh infected inside the meat they serve. When people find out the nature of the woke companies, they will run from them in enormous quantities.

The vaccine manufacturers are also first in line for the distrust. They have conned the people and stolen money without retribution for their killings of the people. There will be massive repeals of liabilities that these companies have enjoyed for years. Big Pharma will find that they will be overtaken by good governance of the Federal Government, until effective managers who have not been tarnished by their evil are found. But that leaves the opportunity for new businesses left and right to take their Cabal counterparts.

Consider the Social Media of Twitter, Facebook and Google (who owns YouTube). They will find that their 230 Protections to call themselves publishing platforms (meaning that they cannot be sued for the material upon the platforms while generally deleting their woke objections) will be deleted. Most will never trust them again. Facebook has blocked me on many occasions. They are so stupid (Q talks of this often) by *indicating* the events of when and how they quelled my TRUTH conversations with the public. That will result in massive fines paid to me and many others.

A company in Tulsa presented their employees with masks and blue gloves on with written pages stating, "we love our patients." This type of woke policy is so out of concert with truth fathomable. The fear derived from wearing garb to protect oneself doesn't resonate with the frequency of love. But people will bring it up to them, until they face their stupid in the face of the criticism. They will struggle to find a balance other than to ignore the past.

How about the Sports franchises of America? You cannot enter Ball Arena in Denver to watch the Nuggets or the Avalanche, unless you show proof of vaccination and wear your mask the whole time. How will they purport to win back the fan base in the face of such lies? How about football stadiums filled with fans required to wear a mask outside but be near one another? The lack of virological protection, if it was a real pandemic, has seeped out of the brains of the businesses who seek to find their footing in a woke culture incorporating the mainstream media bias. But what happens when that bias pushes against them, and the Red Pill opens their lies to truth?

Firstly, as stated earlier, most will function as if they had never believed or operated within the Cabal's lies. They will operate in sports arenas without acknowledgment that they had ever required the fans and the players to be vaccinated against a disease of little deadly consequence. When the withering condemnation reaches the heights of their corporate ears, they will finally post an apology that will ring hollow such as this:

“We wish to apologize to our fans for supporting COVID vaccination procedures that we had believed were in the best interests of the people. But considering the new information presented to our management, we realize that we have lost the people's trust for believing in the lies of the CDC. Please consider coming back to our games, as we reduce ticket prices as an apology for our lack of wisdom in this matter."

The fascination is that big business has always hated competition. When they wish to take over a territory, town or placement of their product, they employ many of the trends stated below:

1. Reduce price below the private businesses' ability to compete.
2. Gain market share and buyout or destroy the competition's ability to compete daily.
3. Then raise the product prices once they have attained a high enough market share of the placement they wished to accomplish.

Or businesses take the following route:

1. Employ lobbyists with severe funds to influence Congress and Senate to do their bidding with millions of slush funds to shut up the opposite message to their desired approach.
2. Create levels of subterfuge to seemingly sneak a bill through by brow-beating the opposing view. Sometimes, this comes in "helping the poor" or other equally appealing qualities filled with lies.
3. See the bill passed and crush their competition with the provisions it could equate for their nefarious purposes.

These methods are always fraught with lies only bought by those Congress and Senate members. They are too easily purchased with the hush money to push the corporate agendas without consideration of small businesses, ethics or moral reservations of the consequences those actions might mean.

How will Corporate Lawyers and Professionals Push these Moral and Ethical Violations to Change Big Business?

In a phrase to answer this question: lawyers and professionals bastardizing their ethical standards in the corporate realms will be a thing of the past. No longer will a young attorney seek the riches of the Big Business to further her career. She will find that butchering her moral compass in the corporate world that needs her expertise to harm their customers without their knowledge will cease to be profitable or honorable. Most of those professionals, including Physicians working for Big Pharma, will find that using their education to subvert justice will be criminal in nature and never practiced again.

I know that sounds like I am moving in a new direction to this question but hear me out. But crime must be punished. When businesses are not allowed to call the authorities for petty crimes (less than $500 thefts), we see that companies fail. Specifically, small businesses cannot afford to lose that much merchandise. It emboldens criminals to loot businesses when they find no teeth to local crime. When people are viewed on videos with masks raiding a pharmacy or grocery store without prosecution, it only leads to greater crime.

When a society chooses to show the penalty

for crime in justice for the laws of the land that are fair (such as the Constitution allows for), criminals will find that they don't want to go to jail. This is something we saw during the riots of 2020. Many don't realize that when ANTIFA and BLM were raiding the cities of America with wanton acts of violence, Trump and the Military were quietly arresting these thugs. They will not be a part of the greatness of NESARA, because all their wealth will not transfer into the new currency, and their property will be seized (EO 13848). Seattle thugs who took over downtown were found afterward were seen with videos of them bawling. There are reports that they had never been punished more than a small fine that George Soros' Group would pay for by their supposedly unlimited funds.

When authorities show that crime is punished after the Red Pill sickos are dealt with, you will find that even the White Collar crimes will be much more brutal to accomplish, because no one wants to be on the lower tier of punishment. If one can't get his managers to cover, as he creates the crime on the ground, the upper managers are weaklings who fold under a bit of pressure from the police. That will trickle down to the corporate world who will have to compete on their merits.

When Big Tech and big corporations, who have never figured out how to truly compete on their merits, endeavor to eke out their own piece of the business pie, they will find that the little guy business owner is beating them in service. Dario Perla is a friend in Gainesville, Georgia with a Clothier shop. He sells suits. But the people love him, because he helps young men figure out who they are in Christ. He wants men to be men of the past with a knowledge of who they were created in God with a purpose to serve God and serve their fellow men. That makes those young men attractive to the opposite sex creating a proper ego.

The value of the actualized service of a Dario Perla will be so apparent to his clientele, while the big corporate fools won't be able to compete on that local level. They won't be able to shuffle the TV media and Social Media (who will have both lost their trust factors in the public eye) with plastic messages that have no value addition. Big businesses will try to overwhelm the crowd with more significant discounts, until they find that the value of the service outweighs the lack that the big corporations can give. It will be a fascinating give and take...taking from the big and giving to the small businesses all completed organically. And those corporate professionals will create their own companies to serve the public, instead of the big overlords.

11
NO TAXATION – HOW PROFITS WILL CHANGE CORPORATIONS

When there are No Corporate Taxes, How Differently will Businesses Operate?

When you delete the IRS inside of Income Taxation, it affects the private sector in many ways (I have earlier dealt with that Income Tax is not needed to run the government). Individuals who don't own a business currently have payroll taxes removed for Federal and State along with Social Security and Medicare. I believe that the withdrawal for Social Security and Medicare will continue, because we will all need that at some later day.

When you own a business, specifically an S Corporation or an LLC, the taxation is more tricky. I have bookkeepers, accountants, and tax accountants, ensuring that profits and expenses are balanced. To offset the taxation, all businesses employ mechanisms to minimize the taxation effect by donating to charities, finding write-offs and other strategies. This deflects profits that are finally summated into a concept called Net Profit. On the other hand, Gross Profit is the calculation of Gross Revenues (all that is sold) minus deletions, returns, and Costs of Goods Sold (COGS). That gives the Gross Profits of the business in which the business owner must pay his/her employees and pay off the general expenses of the month. It does not also calculate one's debt upon the balance sheet but is a monthly check to be written. That's why companies with large debts fail even though their books appear to show enough profit to run the company's expenses.

While that might be more information about running a business than you would ever want to know, the discussion could be relevant as you decide to open your own business in the NESARA era. But without taxation that is calculated on the Net Profit's number, how will that change accounting?

Firstly, as a formal process, Tax Accounting will be a thing of the past. Those same Accountants will find other work doing more accounting of businesses than ever before. The practice of reducing your Net Profit by deflecting write-offs won't be needed which will show a more profitable company than ever known. How much can they afford when that company is more profitable and doesn't have to save for taxation (that comes directly from that owner's pockets)?

Could the company purchase more equipment? Could they hire more employees, which is robust to the economy, increasing the workforce? Could they spend more money on marketing, increasing their market share? When they spend more money, more sales tax revenue that directly benefits that community can be noted for the local governments. There is a difference between small equipment expenditures, like cheaper office chairs, versus Capital Expenditures. When a business feels the lack of constraints upon their budgets, they can think bigger about buying more extensive pieces of equipment (Capital Expenditures) that really grow the economy further because of the increase of purchases. It's a great thing. When more money is spent, more jobs are created.

Value of Money vs. Value of Items

Prices in the economy have always been known to Economists as a relationship between supply and demand. If the supply is high on a product, but the demand is low, the price for that unit becomes saturated, and the price falls. When the demand outstrips the supply of that product, the prices increase dramatically, until it moves above what the "market can bear." That phrase is a different benchmark for each product or service and has many factors. Supply might be high and demand might be increased, but if lousy press comes out about that product or service, the price falls like a rock, as the market readjusts to not wanting that product in the market.

Inflation (the decrease of the value of money) and deflation (the increase of the currency's value) also affect pricing. In 2021, because Joe Biden's criminal policies showed that the Cabal was desperate for cash, they required trillions for their Communist ideals to fund their desires bilking the American public. Those extreme requests of Congress, Senate, and fake Presidency lead to a massive inflation increase. The value of the currency drops as the money floods into the economy without a demand for it. That, thereby, increases the prices to unheard-of levels.

Hyper-inflation is the cliff from which economies fall. The money is so over-abundant that the prices are above the people's heads to afford the basics of life. Then barrels of money cannot buy the minimums, and the people starve. Of course, that's what the Cabal wanted to bring upon the Great Reset that faked out the people that the White Hats were losing to the defunded Cabal. But they absolutely were not. The problem was that the Cabal had the "bullhorn" media in their back pocket decrying anything that wasn't on their Commie agenda.

But when NESARA falls upon the world, Inflation and Deflation become a thing of the past. They were phantoms of the Cabal anyway! The Fiat Currency of the Cabal inside the Central Banks is backed only by the confidence of the market. When the market no longer values the Cabal and its lying principles (another reason the White Hats needed to show the Cabal as liars in 2021), then the new currency of the White Hats of which is projected to be called Rainbow Currency, steps into form the gap that the Fiat left.

Rainbow Currency will be backed by a precious commodity in gold, hence the Gold Standard. Other currencies worldwide will be supported by the precious metals of the country's worth, creating an instant value on the national and international front for the country and the people to create wealth. This process is called GESARA, in which all the countries drop off the Cabal overlords in prisons of their choosing and give back to the people their governmental control.

Then the value of money will rise higher than the world has known for almost a hundred years since the reduction of the Gold-standard buyback of FDR in 1933, I mentioned in previous chapters. When that value of money rises, the price (product) value will decrease. It will create a unique blend of the values falling and money increasing for the people, meaning that more people can afford what they need and want.

People will then need to learn to live within their means. The Greatest Generation and their ancestors knew this lifestyle all too well. They saved for the things they wanted and needed. They didn't invest in the plastic we love (credit cards), because they were seen as evils. They were not that far off! It doesn't mean that credit cards will die in the NESARA era. Far from it. But what it means is that people will need to learn to live with what they make and be more careful. I personally don't carry any cash and pay off my credit cards monthly. Just an easier way to operate my monthly expenses while we live within our means by a budget.

How and When will Prices Fall?

I have thought of little else than this topic during the beginning of this fight to show what

NESARA is about. The Great Reset is the Cabal's trick to raise prices, so that we must live with a new Fiat currency and Communism. It's NOT HAPPENING!

Once the value of the currency takes place inside of NESARA, we first feel the Debt Jubilee, where people see most or all their debts wiped out. Once the euphoria and the shock fades, people begin to get back to work. Prices don't fall at all for a time. Businesses will think that because the people have extra dough to spend, they will continue spending at an accelerated rate after being Red Pilled. They will have the cash and the desire to spend.

But, when the value of money is fully known, then prices through competition will begin to fall. It's hard to drop "Dollar Tree" pricing, but in that case, they will increase to better products for that dollar. Therefore, we will see the reflected purchasing power I mentioned in earlier chapters. The people will also learn to save again in amounts unheard of in the Plastic Debt Economy.

I first heard the term Debt Economy from my friend Will in 2012. He was trying to Red Pill me about the Gold Currency and used Debt Economy liberally. In the Debt Economy, we feel that plastic (credit cards) is king and creates the buying power until we find no more buying power.

People from the poorest to the wealthiest struggle inside the Plastic Economic model. Buy One, Get One Free, or the like creates a frenzy of buying what you don't really need because you were in love with how it made you feel. Only to find that the product wasn't valuable, or you weren't going to put effort into effect to make it worthwhile (i.e., exercise equipment). The purchaser's credit always dries up based upon the debt load and the individual's earning potential or the family. Payment plans and credit usage rises to more than 50%, and then the person feels the crush of the payments needed to outlay for the items purchased. Choices between what is required monthly and what is owed become blurred, until the payment schedules are hijacked to cover the monthly needs. Then the calls come in for payment.

NESARA doesn't release that mentality. But you will find out that what you thought you needed isn't really worth it. It's something that all people will need to quickly learn. Money managers inside of NESARA will need to come out of the woodwork to help people manage their resources efficiently.

Prices will fall firstly for services rendered. Companies such as Massage Therapists have their own overhead and expenses but have few COGS needed to accomplish their practice. The hours in the day and current flow of clients are some of the limitations. But they might find that balance to reduce their price to increase usage. Then the services industry, many as they are, will find an expansion of need to service their demographic effectively. In this case, more and more trained Massage Therapists will be required. But the price will fluctuate until the Supply and Demand stabilize.

Those who have COGS attached to their prices, such as Dario Perla with clothes, will also reduce his pricing, so that more men can purchase his service of tailoring and building up men to be men again in the Biblical fashion as he does. But Dario must work within the strictures of his COGS, and he needs clothes up the supply chain line to realize that it costs less to make the clothes while paying their due.

Prices with COGS will see a slower decline until they stabilize the price quite a bit longer than the service industries. That will also mean that more industries of both types will spring up since the big corporations will be used less and less due to their trust destruction they will incur after the Red Pill.

The Culmination of NESARA on Businesses and you

I would like people to be excited about privatized small businesses. Our society needs to return to that model instead of the corporately-owned facilities. Large firms aren't a part of my issue when they are privately owned. They have directives that they can follow based upon their own desired leadership divisions.

When small and large firms focus on what they do best, they want to serve their customers, whether Biz to Biz (B2B) or Biz to Person (B2P). When the businesses begin to comprehend how to put the clientele's needs first, they will find that service and integrity are not just marketing terms but can be accomplished daily.

God told me to file claims against two massive insurance firms for specific payments that were unrighteously held back. The claims were more than nine months old, and I had had it! We filed numerous times, and the responses were the following: "We don't know why that won't go through, give us ten more days to get it pushed through."

I wrote letters to the Oklahoma Insurance Commission with all the paper documentation on the two separate patient events. I scathingly blasted both insurance carriers for the non-payment, which means I have to be the bank for these idiot firms paying all the expenses. I ended the communication to the state by indicating that the number one message of marketing by insurance and hospitals includes *integrity* when describing what they do. "And they have none."

Before the 20 days were up for one insurance to respond, I received a check in full. The other one went up the chain to a VP in Minnesota. She called me to tell me how to change the invoice numbering (which was never mentioned in any communication for the non-payment) to be paid. She called me back two times to make sure I got paid. Yeah, think I got their attention?

Businesses will learn that integrity is completed by what they do and not what they say. When prices, value, and service converge into one miasma for the business to the clientele, you will see a massive increase in how you are treated daily. Those who cannot compete by doing right by their clientele will cease to exist.

Businesses that cannot care for their employees will find them quitting for better work environments or start up themselves. Government contracts to private firms will be chosen based on merit and ability to complete quickly, not on the good ole boy network or other idiotic choices.

Driving by road work crews is the joke of the American comedian and citizen alike. Three guys standing by while one man digs. What is that about? Businesses will have to complete the jobs efficiently and within budget, or they will never be chosen again for the work will be the norm. Sounds too good to be true?

I am not talking about fantasy here. We are not interacting with Communists or even Democratic ideals that the citizens cannot tame. When you have a Constitutional Republic that demands that the people become involved in their own governance, clarity of purpose becomes the only accepted currency between the interaction groups. From Congress, local municipalities, businesses to the people they all serve. Being left in the cold by inefficiencies will mean you are freezing outside of the process!

12
WHAT ABOUT THE ANGRY FEW?

I haven't painted a rosy picture for you, have I? It will take years to accomplish some of the elements of changes. It will be turbulent at times with complex arguments to be won. Minds will have to be deprogrammed from the Cabal, and even the way we communicate will change. Movies will need to come out with accurate histories that re-educate the stories. I could go on for hours with World Wars and the hidden conflicts.

Rodney Howard-Browne is an engaging pastor in Tampa, Florida. He grew up in South Africa and has lost some of his accent with his years in America. I hadn't heard of him before. I downloaded his book "The Killing of Uncle Sam" on Audible that I *highly* recommend. Firstly, the voice actor is unique with his accents from all over the planet. But Pastor Browne gives extraordinary detail on historical events that I had to research myself. He communicated with me on Twitter after following me, and we have discussed NESARA on a macro scale verifying points with one another. These are the types of histories I recommend for all people to begin to understand how the Cabal has altered our mental landscape to distort history.

But, "Houston, we have a problem."

There will be a number of people who don't want to move into the NESARA era. They will find that their debts are paid off in a way that they could not imagine from their Cabalist Bernie Sanders. Their cash reserves will have been revalued as well. But they are unhappy. They interacted in the gangs of ANTIFA or BLM along with other potentially counter groups.

We are not referring to the criminals within the organization that the White Hats will have already deleted. I am intimating those who were just angry on Social Media and marched upon capitals. These people haven't harmed anyone directly; they just learned their history and swallowed the whale of the Cabal as gospel evidence of the system's sickness.

Many are long-time students at universities or professors of those prominent universities. They spent their lives defending Hillary Clinton and her ilk, shouting down those who would counter their inane arguments that never make any sense to those who aren't emotionally charged. After the Red Pill, it will be challenging to remove this programming by the EBS sending out their messages of silliness of all they believed.

Psychological Harm of Uninformed Beliefs

As we noted above, consider those who have just been through the Red Pill. They received the benefits of the Debt Jubilee. They have a new money that revalues their work more daily.

But they hate the guts of America and all it stands for inside of the Republic. They find new businesses rising from the ashes, and their ANTIFA buddies in prison. They are leaderless and aimless in their pursuits. They have also listened to the EBS broadcasts, until they screamed at the TV to shut up and maybe even threw their shoes through the screens!

Do we have a disconnect, as my wife would say? Yes! They will be the muttering fools on buses and busy malls thinking about spending their new valued currency. They band together as they find their friends who have not gone to federal prison. They will feel persecuted for their beliefs, just as the early Christian church believed in Jesus in China. Someone will rise up with a substantial set of lungs to preach a new message of an uprising.

Each time they attempt a minor coup, the authorities who have pealed off their Cabal overlord oppressors will catch them in the act. They will allow them to congregate, as is their right as citizens of the world, but their illogic will be countered at every turn. They will return harder to the old truths as if they were real. These idiot ANTIFA kids will bring the old literature they recruited back into vogue in those underground meetings.

How do we counter them? The new media will begin to investigate like they were supposed to in the past. I see the lack of plastic-looking men and women with perfectly cut faces deleted from the screen. Replaced will be usual-looking reporters who can communicate what they have investigated. Many may be from the Q movement and had huge followings on the Social Media channels now employed on the large new networks for Patriots.

Truth will be our only weapon for these unfortunates. But even Q noted that 4-6% of those will never come back:

1. *Q3029 on March 11, 2019 – 4-6% [brainwashed] will never wake up even when present w/FACTS.*
2. *Q529 on January 13, 2018 - ....Fake News, 4-6% lost forever...*
3. *Q337 on December 13, 2017 - ....Estimated 4-6% we consider 'hopeless' and forever brainwashed. (8)*

Churches in their own Pile of Lies

What do you do for the Churches? Pray for them. Here is the truth you will find inside of this example: Steve is also an Associate Pastor of a local church.

Just after the Red Pill, a congregation will stumble into a church in droves, surprising the pastor. He tended to note eighty families in attendance but cannot believe the one hundred and fifty that gather that they could get out next Sunday. The head pastor will have prepared a message of hope before the Red Pill but feels shaky at his lectern that Sunday morning. He hadn't investigated either what the world was facing with the Cabal.

Before he can even fully introduce his morning topic, one of the new attendee's bolts to his feet and insistently requests that the pastor explain how the Bible is relevant to what the EBS refers to. "Pastor, we need truth. I have only spent a few minutes inside of the Bible. Now, I realize that I have wasted my time with you. How did the EBS change what we should believe? I mean, what's happening in the world? Who do we believe?" The desperate man is honestly searching for truth, as he slides back down in his seat. The pastor mumbles through some comments about what he has learned from the broadcasts but has no real answers since he is processing his own shock.

Realize that many churches will lose their congregation almost overnight, because they have supported the Democratic candidate such as the fraudulent Joe Biden or Barack Obama or supported the BLM agenda while using the Bible to claim those truths. One pastor last year even exclaimed from a Tulsa pulpit, "Thank God we don't have a spirit of fear with COVID, but thank Jesus for the vaccine!"

Those messages will be deemed a lie, and there will be no returning to the grace of his people with the deceits he embraced. On the other hand, others ignorant of the Red Pill revelations will promise to investigate the truths that were birthed with her congregation. She will find a kinship she can cultivate if she fully adopts new supposed Conspiracy Theories, she hadn't accepted beforehand.

But most will have to bow out of their position, because they really weren't accepting the Bible as the Word of God. Truth vacated their preaching long ago. Faced with objective truth and a demand *for* truth from his people, he will not be able to meet the criticism he knows is coming.

Dave is an older man here in Tulsa whom I didn't remember meeting before my first Hope Conference with Pastor Sherlock Balley (we do conferences together on End Time events). Dave was praying over his church and reported that, because so many people prayed over some of the sections of the church that the Spirit of God was super strong in those portions of the sanctuary. I was highly focused on my presentation, so I just took his word for it.

Dave was patient and listened to our four-hour presentation between Dr. Sherlock and me. Then he came to one of my meetings at my office where we were going to talk on the *Truth and Lies of What We Believe* series (basically, the hardest questions of the Bible), but I sensed a powerful calling of God to talk about much of the information within this book! Dave stared back at me, as if I were an alien the whole time.

HE CAME UNGLUED after I put some memes on Facebook against the vaccine. It became a long-running diatribe against all the people in the Church, killing others for not receiving the vaccine as he had proudly injected into his body. It became on the level of verbal abuse before I shut him down and banned him from my sites. He gave Scriptures supporting his paranoia on COVID and the official narrative believing all he heard from the Mainstream Media.

The Angry's Response to Truth

How will these people respond after they hear the truth on COVID, the Vaccine, Pedophilia all over our nation at the highest levels, and the satanism the Cabal performs? Some will have a clue that it was real. I know many who dabble on the Conspiracy side of the fence, while not rocking their friend's boat upon Vaccines. They actually got their shots out of fear and responded in kind to that fear in other situations.

Others will hear the truth as if for the first time, and they will not feel the spiritual tuning to the frequency of truth. Does that sound strange to mention? Without getting off into a tangent here, I need to reference a Scripture: "But now, apart from the law, God's righteous has been revealed – attested by the Law and the Prophets – that is, God's righteousness through faith in Jesus Christ, to all who believe, since there is no distinction." Romans 3:21-22. How does that refer to the topic at hand?

God's Righteousness is the absolute standard by which we live in His presence. It's not "I'm good enough," but am I perfect? My righteousness is deleted by that level perfection that the Law of God reveals (meaning that the Law was just supposed to show you can't accomplish it). The only way to attain the level of Righteousness that the Father requires is through belief in Jesus and what He did.

But there is a word buried in the text that no one pays any attention to which is Distinction (*Diastole).* To know the difference between Jesus and us as we accept what Jesus really offers in His truth is that *Diastole.* It's what only a musician can hear in the distinction of two notes.

My wife and son were playing *Wii Music* when he was much younger, as I was studying the book of Romans in a new fashion approximately a dozen years ago. One of the challenges in the game was to note which instrument was making a particular pitched note. In musical terms, it means Timbre. The tone that a guitar makes when it hits a middle C is radically different than a banjo in the same note because of the strings and the physical function of the two instruments. As a musician and singer myself, I know this intuitively. I can't stand it when someone is slightly out of tune, which is one of the reasons I am so picky with what I listen to. I have that level of *Diastole* in my musical choices.

The Angry has been operating under a set of rules for truth. They wish to interact with those who purvey their truth (resonant) through an authority. It's the worst set of logic known to understand truth. Because I am an authority on a topic doesn't mean that I am right! Truth functions on a plane that it doesn't matter who presents it; it can stand upon its own two feet without care to the orderly condition of the speaker. That's why I gravitate toward *Veritas* truth that I can verify. But Scripturally, we must intermittently interact in other ways with the truth.

"He who saw this has testified so that you also may believe. His testimony is true, and he knows he is telling the truth (John 19:35)." The very first time I interacted with this verse in college, I remember how I felt about it as an English major: it needed a rewrite of the wording! But you must break down the words (I will shorten this teaching without giving you the full details).

John had witnessed the Crucifixion in his writing that came much later than the other Gospels knowing that there was already a severe amount of criticism within the church for the belief in a resurrection and death event. In effect, John stipulated that he would bear witness of his testify (Martyeo), meaning he would die for placing his hands on the Bible before he gave his witness (something that happened in court years ago). His testimony (*Martyria*) is the evidence he presents in the court case that is true (*Alethinos*) or the opposite of a fiction John was writing. And when John ends with telling the truth (*Alethes*) he indicates that he loves the truth. Therefore, as if he were presenting a court case that he would die for the testimony, he was suggesting that he would die for the words he spoke that were untrue.

The Book of John's level of truth is unquestioned which is why I believe in the whole Bible (in those above verses, I can prove that the Bible has never been rewritten in a forty-five-minute session, and no one has destroyed that point yet). When the people of the planet hear that level of testimony from the White Hats with the criminal Cabal admitting to their crimes with the corroborating evidence, they will struggle with that kind of non-fiction telling, since they are so unfamiliar with truth produced in that manner.

It's going to be a rocky ride for those who cannot come to the truth on their own. We will be required to repeatedly re-tell the Red Pill event's stories for these angry people who can't seem to grasp it in the first go-round! But when they do get it, they will be grateful that you spent the time in their lives (maybe not at the moment that might be filled with the F word hurled from their gut in which Satan has resided for a long time) to give them the truth. Pray! Know what you need to say.

13

A PROPHETIC VIEW AFTER THE RED PILL OF OUR FUTURE

I had a captivating conversation with a group of Patriots in my office that we try to do every Thursday night. Most, if not all, are believers in Christ. It's illuminating what they are asking and what they have researched. Wendy takes a ton of notes and pushes out assignments, so that we can all examine the Cabal evidence together.

I presented two separate *fictional* cases of couples. The first couple, Steve and Deb, make 90K together yearly. They have a house that they owe $250K and $80K of debts. Because of their debt load at this time, they can't save, since they haven't deemed it terribly effective. Their obligations are high, and they live a lifestyle trying to keep up with the purchases they and their kids might want/need. They, therefore, only have $1500 in savings.

The second couple, Frank and Jane, have lived within their means for many years. They also make $90K between them. But instead, they have only $5000 in debt, something that they are ready at any moment to pay off. Frank and Jane also have $350K in their stocks, $20K in gold and $50K in cash/savings. They are well on their way to retirement and know how to save.

Who is in better shape once the Red Pill with the Debt Jubilee occurs? Most would rightly say that Steve and Deb (the first couple) would be. On the surface, that's correct. But let's take a closer look at Steve and Deb.

Debt-Based Couple

Our fictional Steve and Deb find that NESARA turns their credit report upside down. Instead of fighting at 620 credit ratings that put them at a higher risk for debt loads and $80K of cars/credit card debt, not to mention their $250K of a house loan, that $330K is gone! They are partying in the streets with their champagne bottles. They tell their friends on Social Media after recovering from the shock of all the Cabal stories of Trump and the White Hats have done for them. They will also come to realize that a credit score is meaningless in the impact of no Debt by which one of the main factors in creating a debt to income scoring system.

But Steve and Deb haven't learned what moving into the cash/asset-backed economy means. They purchased numerous goods with credit cards in the past, not caring if they could pay that 90" TV off for the upstairs game room that they really don't need, but Steve likes to see the NFL in massive HiDef 8K. Once they find that they can have cleaned out credit cards by the White Hats, they wonder what they can purchase now, since they have just begun to hear about NESARA with the cash economy instead of the debt-based economy model.

They also begin to rejoice that no more money is taken out in their paychecks for the IRS in Fed and State taxation. It's all a little confusing but exciting at the same time. They begin to feel flushed with spending money they didn't have in the past. They would constantly fight if Steve purchased that upstairs TV that Deb didn't think they needed. Deb was trying to get into shape again and wanted to get the newest workout concept of these mirrors that talked you through interacting with others.

At first, they carefully begin to spend and find that they can somewhat afford what's going on in the household budget. But they start to hear about budgeting for the NESARA era but can't really imagine what it entails, since they have never operated within a budget other than paying the bills.

When they approach the bank in about a year of ignoring their budget plans about a new loan to consolidate the debt that begins to rise, they find that the same bank they have approached in the past is redescent to offer attractive rates for paying off their debts. They still haven't realized to live within their means. Sure, they put a tax refund from the previous year in savings, so they now have $4000 in it, but they removed a little for some yard work.

The fights begin as the budget squeeze gets tighter, and they haven't learned that debt is really a problem when *Cash is King*, as the old motto from the previous century rears its descriptive head. How are they going to find another way to pay their debts down?

Cash-Based Couple

Frank and Jane are pleased as punch that the $5000 came off the books. They had found a way to inherit the small house from their parents that they loved to fix up and make it beautiful. Their industriousness has been a passion in their life. But they find people like Steve and Deb in their church who claim that their massive debts were paid off, even finding out the forgiven amounts.

Two emotions emerge within Frank and Jane without realizing it. Firstly, they are joyous with their friends that the world of evil has been lifted from their chests, and they praise God for that. Secondly, they are secretly jealous that the Fed death killed off Steve and Deb's massive debts, because Frank and Jane hadn't received the same number of debt forgiveness. Frank and Jane always lived within their means and worked hard. But something else comes up in their research that they didn't believe at first: their cash assets are becoming more valuable, allowing their purchasing power to increase exponentially (which says nothing of the interest rates they are earning upon the money they have saved). That understanding of the assets creates more impotence to save than ever before.

After approximately a year of keeping their own pace in savings, all their assets have dramatically risen in value. It had been a dream to maybe replace the old house that they had put care into, but they hated the idea of significant debt. Suddenly, as they perceive the market on housing, all the homes are significantly cheaper. With the increased assets on hand, they pay in cash to purchase the dream house they feel could even retire within several years. They spend all they purchase monthly, even if they use a credit card to buy it. They are giving more away in the church. Because of their understanding of wealth management and even teaching Deb and Steve how to begin to build their life in an asset-backed economy, the church approaches them to teach money and savings more than old teachings of how to pay off their debts.

New Thinking on Money

"For the love of money is a root of all kinds of evil, and by craving it, some have wandered away from the faith and pierced themselves with many pains (I Timothy 6:10)." When I discuss NESARA on my YouTube channel, it never fails that someone quotes only a part of this verse. "The love of money is the root of evil..." pushed out to denigrate even the *evil* conversations about currency, bringing the Bride of Christ inside the greedy bugger's metaphor.

But think of the above verse for a little bit. The ROOT (Rhiza) indicates that the offspring of the love of the money causes germination of thought that takes people away from our faith. What firstly springs to mind are the TV evangelists that you have doubtless heard who have based themselves in the world and Masonic teaching, eschewing the Word of God. They "wandered" away from Christ to pursue money that should only consider a conduit or vehicle.

It's fascinating to note that the rich and poor of the Debt-Based Society will be moving out of their old way of thinking daily about wealth. The super-wealthy laugh at the poor who pay little in taxes, but the Poor pay another type to the wealthy: the Lottery. The illusory winning of millions sinks cash that the poor never have enough of. But when the Cabal Uber wealthy are jailed or died for their sick ritualistic abuses on many levels, how will that all change in our world's concept of money?

Most will need to rethink their values of cash or the pursuit of it. *We were never made to sink what we don't have to buy what we don't need.* I have done that at times, only to glance back with disgust at the inane purchases made in the stupidity of my cravings. It may take a generation of releasing us from the lifelong curse of the debt-based economic approach that money managers were only spouting what they learned in their licensure tests and the wealth managers above them.

Moments of Unrest and The Matrix

Change, even meaningful change, does not come with open arms of those within it. Consider the movie mentioned above, *The Matrix,* completed in 1999. Morpheus, the character Neo reveres for his escape from the

Matrix and his fake life, sacrifices himself in another escape to save Neo again. Trinity, their partner in the flight for Neo, who also falls in love with Neo, is told to get him to safety since Zion (a city outside the Matrix underground the earth's surface). The next two movies in the original series interact with Neo's unique abilities to protect them from the machine world of the Matrix.

Again back in the first movie, Morpheus is chained to an old rolling chair with electrodes upon his forehead measuring his EEG response to stimuli. Mr. Smith, an authorized representative of the Machine Mainframe, is sent to control the people, as he questions Morpheus and reveals secrets of the past approximately one hundred years since the machines have taken over the planet, harvesting humans as a power source without the sun. The sun was sacrificed during the human vs. machine war in which humans had launched a massive series of nuclear weapons destroying the atmosphere to contaminate the machines from their power source.

Mr. Smith admits that the Mainframe authority had created a virtual paradise for the people they plugged into the Matrix in their first incarnation of the virtual world. It was perfect, almost with Garden of Eden references, but the people rejected it. After several variables accounted for in future machinations of the computer world, they settled upon the world of the late 20th century with crime and corruption. That's what humans would gravitate to with comfort, knowing that things aren't always fair.

I am sorry to give you a detailed response within the above information if you had watched *The Matrix* series, but it's precious to consider. When people are released from this "movie" that Q talks of it as, we are going to find that many are wholly unprepared for this new reality no matter how nice it is not to have the following: debt, IRS taxation, corrupt politics, unfair legal practices and sick high-profile idols in all places of the boob tube.

They will not be able to readily admit that it was wrong. As we discussed in earlier chapters, Chaos will still be somewhat of the norm. It's not just rioting that will be occurring, but ultimately, new conversations moving in and out of churches, lecture halls, pubs, and restaurants. Old biases of the Democrat and Republican, Left and Right, and racial tensions that became a blanket to wrap one's philosophic Matrix around will disappear in a blink of an eye. Listen, racism and these other problems still exist, but the focus will be on dividing and conquering what the Cabal loves to do to populations. No longer will we be able to parse out silly group-think truths by authority just because the speaker wishes to.

People will question what all are stating, which causes professional and personal angst in jobs and businesses worldwide that operate upon that piss poor basis of logic: "Trust me, I know what I am talking about." Many of those institutional trusts will be gone.

Disappearing Institutional Trust

Once we find that Physicians were not researching why the vaccines were killing, creating autism in children, and a host of other crippling diseases without the concomitant effects of increased health, hospitals and Physicians' offices will find a distrust that might bring those institutions to their knees. The American Medical Association (AMA) will be found to be a part of the Cabal for their work against humanity, along with the Centers for Disease Control (CDC) in their games with big pharma. How will people respond to those who didn't do wrong but are still Physicians or health care workers in those facilities? Their influence will be questioned, and those people will need to learn to regain the public's trust. Many of those hospitals and insurance institutions might falter to the point of closure. That may not be a bad thing. But it's uncomfortable.

How about Money Managers? They were the ones who *didn't* tell us about the Fiat Currency, and how evil the debt-based structure was. They didn't warn us about NESARA and how it would positively impact the world. Mantras, such as Death and Taxes, will be a thing of the past that those money institutions propagated.

As I mentioned in the first chapter, the SEC claimed that banks were the most righteous type of institution it knows. This fraudulent and ruinous statement may even bring that sick organization to its death kneel along with many of the big banks. As I discussed earlier, don't worry; you will have time to take your money out. But those jobs will have to be replaced in our economy, and that doesn't happen overnight! This brings me to the point I would love to make to each person: Move out of the big old banks and go to your local banks where relationships matter!

Working for the Public Good as it happens as a Mayor, Governor, Senator, or Congress will have little charm and glory. Those who have not participated in the system's sickness, which will be precious few, might have to defend even stating that "I was a Senator...but a Patriot!" New ones who go in will have new battle cries to keep their ears to the public desires, so that they represent what is needed in their community.

Media will take on a new light. They might be a little more in your face finding out the sickest portions of our world. Investigative reporting will have to be honest and uncovering. Most of it has been so lacking at searching out truth, because their bosses have lost sight that they are the bastions of the society to inform on the secrets that governments are doing. Both Media and Government need to *fear* and *respect* the people in all their decisions. If they don't, the media's new job (but original purpose) is to expose those corruptions and show the people the potential problem. The law must also fill in the blanks where the Media watchdog ends.

Lawyers and judges will be harshly criticized for betraying the people's trust. They have marginalized the Constitution that they were initially created to protect their arguments and decisions. They were not to recriminate the Constitution, allowing governance to bastardize it with lying flare! They will, too, find that many of their ranks will be rotting in prison or found at the end of a noose.

Their professors and mentors in the halls of higher learning were the sickos that the lawyers and judges were meant to protect the public who didn't understand the nature of the Constitutional law that needed a representative against Institutional Corruption. They failed in their academic roles and must learn to beg the public to trust them again.

Teachers and professors will need to pull back from the inane logic that has been absent from their classrooms for so many dozens of years. Some will not be able to do so and will have to retire from that line of work. Children and young adults must openly question the logic trails of their adults in charge. Parents will need to challenge the schools and universities, until they model their ideals upon truth and not radical viewpoints that are not foundational to consummate learning.

My father used to talk about getting degrees in Underwater Basket Weaving. He was referring to the useless degrees that do not have a place in society, and they are Woke topics built in the lies of the Cabal. Those kids need to retrain themselves in a field of study that might further the world and have some level of truth within it.

These public institutions will learn that only patent honesty will convince their consumers of their intellectual goods that their position deserves to remain. They will all need to adjust their thinking. Many might need to attend night school just for coursework that retrains their thought processes in new ways of serving the people they were originally meant to serve. No longer will they trust an institution's bodies without questioning their authorities of why and how they can support a claim that the teachers make.

14
Real Eschatology

A Fictional Tale of Perspective

I need to wade into Eschatology for a bit, which is the study of End Times from a Biblical perspective. Many Patriots currently feel strongly that we are living in the Tribulation period. They view Scriptures here and there while trying to prove we are inside the Tribulation right now. I will not denigrate my brothers and sisters in Christ but use one nameless person.

One woman big in the Patriot community (of whom I like much of her research on Patriot issues) purported in her book that the Rapture was a myth. She also stated that the Tribulation is not seven years. She doesn't PROVE her point but stipulated it, as if it were evident that the idea is false. She flushed approximately six hundred Scriptures under the rug in one felled-swoop without even a casual glance. The ones she does examine a little further are proof of the moment we are living in Biblical times, meaning NESARA and the end of this time of corruption. Let's explain how much out of context it might be.

Let's say I was the Offensive Coordinator of a prominent High School team in your area. We have had a two-week training camp, and you are the local reporter tasked with covering the team. The problem is that you know so very little about football, because the two that surrounded the team are out on vacation. The article must be done now.

You travel to the practices and gain permission to write an in-depth story of the inner workings of our amazing football team who has won glory in the state three years in a row. The readers want to know how. But you come about one week into practice. After finding out the relevant people related to the team, you use your phone to record some of the instructions I give to my players.

"Dang guys (cuss word excluded)! You make me sick. Blow that guy away! Kill 'em...humiliate 'em..."

That night you are reviewing the transcripts you had. You can't really remember where they were in context to the day as you sit upon the Motel Six bed that is always a little too squishy by the end table. But you repeatedly listen to his brazen philosophy presented to young minds of a coach who has won the state three years running with his innovative offense, or so you have heard. But again, you don't really understand football or coaching that much.

You believe there is a story in the wording here. You blast this Offensive Coordinator being a narcissist and conniving the youth of this small town to literally kill their opponents. You blow the story up into the ills against violence against women. Proud of your account and believing that it will be the start of a new career uncovering the converting of our youth into a life of murder, your editor screws her face up, as she reads your detailed column you have expanded into ten pages with a series in mind.

"James, do you really understand football and what that coach might have been saying?" your editor Sheldon asks you as she pulls down her glasses only partway through your article.

"I think it's plain as day, don't you?" confused by the reaction you retort.

Who is the Bride of Christ?

The above fictional story indicates how little some Patriots have studied End Time issues related to the Bible. I am not talking about the Koran, which has much to say about an End Time that Muslims believe. Nope, I am talking about the Christian viewpoint that should be focused on as the prophetic guidance manual.

To explain it in a very succinct fashion. There will be an End Time. We are the Bride of Christ and fulfill Jesus in His need to marry His Bride, so He, therefore, comes for her, as it relates to the Jewish tradition of a seven-day wedding feast that begins with a consummation and ceremony of matrimony. After which, the Wedding Feast continues for the above seven days (seven years), and they live in the city with the house he has built for her for one year as the community supports them in that first year (one thousand years) of marriage.

We are the Bride of Christ in Scripture. We are not the children...we are not the Sheep. We are the Bride. Jesus doesn't return to the planet to marry a little girl. That would be the pedophilia way of the world, as I explained in earlier chapters. That's what Satan wishes to do in how he treats children. Nope, the children need to grow up. Those who come to Christ are as children to Him. They know nothing. They are similar to the Sheep who just hear His voice but are not wise in the ways of the Word and what Jesus wants for His Bride.

After they get to know Jesus through the Word that the Holy Spirit presents in the sixty-six books with only forty authors (there are no hidden books of the Bible), they grow up. One matures by understanding more of their position in Christ, similar to what a child does as she learns who she is and takes her place in the world. Paul states that as a child, I thought like a child...but now as an adult, I think like an adult (I Corinthians 13:11). That means as we grow up, we become the Bride. So easy, isn't it? That's why Jesus comes back for you BEFORE the Tribulation to fulfill the wedding vow He made!

Tribulation

When one thinks of the Apocalypse, they think of that End Time foretelling in Scripture. But that's not what it means in Greek, no matter what the dictionaries say about it in English! Apocalypse means Revelation or an unveiling, and it does not mean that everything blows up!

The Tribulation is referred to throughout the New Testament, specifically in Revelation 6-19. But it has its origins in Daniel 9:27. "He will make a firm covenant with many for one week, but in the middle of the week, he will put a stop to sacrifices and offering…" Who the heck is he? That's the Anti-Christ. Many verses spend quite a bit of time upon him. As we have already explained, he is a person and will be revealed by Jesus in Revelation 6. The Cabal doesn't get to introduce him; Satan doesn't get to introduce him…only Jesus!

When Daniel explains the verse of "one week," we realize he talks about seven years throughout the book, which can be a little hard to fathom. But there are many veiled references within the writings. Therefore, the Tribulation starts with the Anti-Christ, as he brings a peace treaty with many (nations) for the peace of Israel. But he comes with a bow and no arrows seeking to conquer (which means authority without the governmental might, in the beginning, to do so).

Some mistakenly believe that Trump brought a peace treaty for Israel inside NESARA. He did NOT do that. Trump brought a peace treaty with almost every single nation. It wasn't about Israel; it was about the whole world. It wasn't about a multinational approach; it was to bring about the end of the Cabal.

But if you believe that we were in the Tribulation in 2020 and even in 2024, you got another thing coming. Let's give a couple points that you cannot replicate with what's happened in the world, shall we (I will not cover every one of the twenty-one judgments recorded in Revelation)?

1. Second Seal – Red Horse of a massive war I would deem as World War III, which occurs in the first half of the Tribulation (still believe that the first half of the Tribulation is peaceful?).
2. Third Seal – Hyper-Inflation without harming the rich. Great Reset would have done that. This will be regenerated again when the Anti-Christ takes over, and NESARA is killed. Yes, it will die when the Anti-Christ takes over.
3. First Trumpet – Hail, Fire and Blood from heaven burn one-third of the earth's grass.
4. Third Trumpet – Massive star falls into the sea to poison the waters.
5. Fourth Trumpet – Diming of stars, moon and sun by one-third may be due to the comet that comes into the sea?
6. Fifth Trumpet – people without the seal of God are stung but cannot die for five months. That means we may have zombie-type responses (read my book on DrScottYoung.com, "Our Secret Zombie Life") of people who try to kill themselves but can't die for those five months.
7. Second Bowl – All seas are turned to blood.
8. Third Bowl – Freshwaters are turned to blood.
9. Seventh Bowl – Massive earthquake that takes down islands and every mountain.

So, I ask you in just a cursory reading of the above judgments of God, have they happened yet? If your answer is NO to every one of these, then we haven't seen the beginning of the Tribulation, to say nothing of the middle of the Tribulation. The Sixth Trumpet (I didn't include that above) might be known as World War IV, killing more than two-thirds of the planet in about one year.

My wife and I state it this way when people ask if 2020-2021 were the Tribulation as some Patriots exclaim: If you think we are in the Tribulation now, multiply that number by about one thousand, and you might be close to how wrong that time will be. No, we are absolutely, positively not in the Tribulation.

Millennial Reign or 1000 Years of Peace

Without even talking about the Tribulation, some Patriots claim we are experiencing; they then believe that NESARA will usher one thousand years of peace. They have no idea that Scripture uses more than three hundred verses to explain that timeframe of which Abraham was dreaming as his point of Faith in Hebrews 11.

Abraham was told of a time (in Genesis) in which his descendants would number as many as the sand of the seashore. Just a rough estimate here, but that might be a number of Jews numbering in the billions. Since that hasn't happened, realize that Abraham believed by Faith in something that would *not* happen in his lifetime. I know you might have lost hope (your feeling of the here and now), but Faith is "the evidence of things hoped for and the promise of things unseen (Hebrews 11:1)."

Uh, I don't think that has happened yet! The Millennial Reign only starts when the Anti-Christ, False Prophet, and Satan are put into the Abyss (through the Millennial Reign, after which time when only Satan is removed for another short time), and Jesus is seen in the clouds for the whole world. Jesus sets up His kingdom in Jerusalem, and King David becomes the governor of Israel. Since those things have a bit of time before they are a reality, Patriots believing we are almost in the Millennial Reign will be disappointed.

The Tribulation must have the last temple built in Jerusalem that has to be defiled by the Anti-Christ, which hasn't happened. But then the Millennial Reign will have a Temple that will stretch out for one hundred and fifty miles wide to accommodate all the people on the planet who will come up for the Feast of Tabernacles each year, which means that they tell stories of what the Lord has done for them (see my book series on "ForeTold book one and two" on DrScottYoung.com).

This future time will be of peace, because Jesus is on the throne, and we, His Bride and others, are ruling and reigning with Him in the Heavenlies with our new bodies. Since I don't feel a new body with my bad knees, you can't tell me that has happened yet.

Revelation as Allegory

When I point out the flaws in some Patriot Christians and non-Christians' viewpoints on the Tribulation and the Millennial Reign

Biblically, they point to another weak bullet in the chamber akin to placing a 25-caliber shell in a nine-millimeter. Doesn't work, does it?

Some Patriots claim that the book of Revelation shouldn't be taken literally, and it's an extended Allegory of which we can see parallels, "because I saw a guy on YouTube explain it that way!" So, does the guy on YouTube bring you into Heaven with his ability to translate you to Jesus? If the answer is no, it's the opposite mentality that the man on YouTube is trying to make a point creating a fictional reality without understanding the Word of God.

Each time I hear a person claim that Revelation and those Eschatology Scriptures all over the New Testament and the Old Testament are allegories or metaphors, they follow it up with proof that the verse is talking about whatever they wish it to be (read above just a portion of those Scriptures of the twenty-one judgments to realize that they are INCREDIBLY detailed to NOT be allegories). That means all of it is up for interpretation, and let's move that kind of logic to its final destination.

Suppose (just for a moment) that the book of Revelation is an Allegory of an extended nature. In that case, other parts of the Bible are too that are hard to understand, such as the following: Daniel, Ezekiel, Isaiah, the beginning of Genesis in the Creation account, Zachariah, Matthew 25/26/27, Luke 12, II Thessalonians 2:2-12, I Thessalonians 4:16-19, and I Corinthians 15 to name just a few. If those are not what they seem and open to stating that they are not to be taken literally, where do we stop? Do we say that Paul indicated that “All have sinned and fallen short of Christ (Romans 3:23) or “The wages of sin is death, but the gift of God is eternal life through Christ Jesus” (Romans 6:23) would also be placed in the above allegorical categories? If those are true, then do we have to believe anything in the Bible? Indeed, we can skip the part about Jesus rising from the dead! Yeah, that works! I could go on.

I came home for a holiday in college in the 1980s. My parents and I were sitting in the hot tub outside in the gorgeous elements. When the snow fell around you, it was glorious to sit in for forty-five minutes only at the water's one hundred and one-degree temperatures. It was a time when I could talk to friends or my parents about things I was learning about God. On one of those weekends, my dad quipped that he could believe everything about Jesus in the Gospels except for that difficult section of Him rising from the dead.

“Then dad, forget it all...none of it would have any meaning!”

“No, that’s not what I am saying!” he responded not to offend as well as indicating he believed the rest of the claims of Jesus’ First Coming. But Paul backs my position up! If you cannot be convinced that Jesus rose from the dead, then we should be “pitied among all men (I Corinthians 15:19-20 note that I mentioned this Scripture above in my dissertation about the veracity of the Word).”

If we get to pitch the things we don’t like in the Word, because they are uncomfortable, where does it stop? It does NOT stop until we have marginalized the Word of God. In my classes on the Truth and Lies of What We Believe (the hardest questions of the Bible), I state this point.

"Note that Genesis is attacked by scientists as the stupid Creation story with no scientific foundation as opposed to the basis that Evolution has (of course, we can poke holes in that one too). Another area of contention is the people throughout the last two thousand years who disprove by their unbelief the death or resurrection of Jesus. Then we also have people who marginalize Revelation or the end of the world.

"If we get to skip the beginning of the book, that pesky middle section of the Resurrection, and then the ending in Revelation, how valid is the middle? Who benefits from this tearing up of the Word of God? Satan! He is the great book critic of all time. He has read the Bible cover to cover, and he has carefully picked apart those sections with which he wishes to kill off. If a book is invalid in the beginning, middle, and end, how valid is it in totality? How much work do I have to do to beat up Daniel's idea existing in the Old Testament? None at all."

Do you see? You cannot marginalize Revelation to suit your needs of the now. You cannot take the eternal (the Words of God) and place it inside the temporary (situations you see on the news), because they appear close to one another! The revelations of the Word of God will be exactly as they were when Jesus died and rose from the dead. There are over six hundred

Scriptures in the Old Testament that Jesus perfectly and precisely fulfilled. Jesus was that precise! It made the chance of Jesus not matching the prophesied Messiah (means Savior in Aramaic) more infinitesimal than evaluating the hair samples of every person who has ever lived and only finding one full blue-haired person.

So, What is the NESARA timeframe from a Biblical View?

I believe that there are two probabilities. And even with my extensive research, I am leaving those possibilities out for Jesus to reveal something I hadn't thought of, and it's His plan, as I concede in my writing.

Number one is that it fulfills the Old Testament predictions and the New Testament forecasts of a time when the money is returned to the people along with the Debt Jubilee. I believe that Jesus wishes to extend grace to adding more people into the Kingdom of God before He opens the First Seal to start the Tribulation (of which I pray you are a part of the Bride of Christ and are gone with me).

Number two, NESARA, and the anti-corruption element indicate what I heard and saw when I was in my Near Death Experience (*Near Diagnosis Experience: I was brought back for the Storm* on DrScottYoung.com). I explained it a bit earlier. We will "only see it with our eyes and witness the punishment of the wicked (Psalms 91:8)." These people are evil to the core. When you investigate the nature of thirty-third degree Freemasons, you will find that most massively popular people in government, Hollywood or Media are top-level Masons.

These people openly hate Jesus and all He stands for. They also hate you! You are the “vulgar,” meaning vile and ordinary, and you are meant to service their needs. If the Cabal really had control, they would not end the world, as the Bible claims we would move to in the End Time. Matthew 24:22 “Unless those days were limited, no one would survive. Therefore, if one day were added to the Tribulation, all flesh would be dead! But those days will be limited because of the elect.”

No, the Cabal would pair the planet down to approximately five hundred million people through war, disease and vaccines. Those left would service them through their sexual desires or be the worker slaves of the planet seeking their masters to provide them with all they need at subsistence levels, and no more than that.

Satan in 2020 wanted to bring about the end of the world. When they think like the Cabal, many of the Patriots could reckon that concept with the evidence the Cabal was pushing outward. They wanted the vaccine of COVID to be the miracle Mark of the Beast. BUT, the Cabal wanted to be the *Beast* that would rule the world. They tried to reinterpret Scripture to meet their needs. If they were allowed to do so by allegory or metaphor, they would have invalidated the Word’s claims that the world would end in the fashion that the Tribulation through the nearly seven hundred verses indicates.

If that happened, God would become a liar in the face of Satan and his plans. Of course, that's what Satan wants. He wants to be elevated to God's position, of which Satanism and Freemasonry (two sides of the same coin) postulate that he is the only God of this universe and that the Father is the usurper. But God said NO! During the Tribulation of the future, Satan will be hurled out of Heaven in Revelation 12 with the following curse to the earth "Woe to you for the devil has come down with great wrath knowing that his time is short."

You have it! Revel in this next NESARA time. We will spread the Good News throughout the world, because they will be hungry for the truth.

References

1. *Code of Ethics Exhibit 14.2 created by the SEC* https://www.sec.gov/Archives/edgar/data/706863/000095015610000097/ex14_74905.htm
2. Federwisch (2006), *Ethical Issues in the Financial Services Industry* https://www.scu.edu/ethics/focus-areas/business-ethics/resources/ethical-issues-in-the-financial-services-industry/
3. Bayly (2020), *Former head of Wells Fargo banned from banking after role in sales scandal* https://www.nbcnews.com/business/business-news/former-head-wells-fargo-banned-banking-after-role-sales-scandal-n1121396
4. History.com Editors (2020), *Troubled Asset Relief Program (TARP)*, https://www.history.com/topics/21st-century/troubled-asset-relief-program
5. Bernard (2009), *Bailed-out banks gave millions in exec bonuses, NY AG report shows*, https://abcnews.go.com/Business/story?id=8214818&page=1
6. *Gold Standard: A Currency's value in gold, https://corporatefinanceinstitute.com/resources/knowledge/economics/gold-standard/*
7. Greaves (1995), *How to Return to the Gold Standard, The Major Obstacle to Monetary*

Reform is Ideological, https://fee.org/articles/how-to-return-to-the-gold-standard/

8. Q The World is Watching, Intelligence Drops, https://qalerts.app/?q=4-6%25

ABOUT THE AUTHOR

Dr. Scott Young, CCC-A, FAAA, an Audiologist since 1991, and owns Hearing Solution Centers, Inc. in Tulsa, OK. Besides World War II studies, his passions include writing, Sci-Fi and singing. He has authored a fictional novel, *The Violin's Secret*, which chronicles the survival of one young teenager through the Holocaust.

ForeTold - Book 1 and 2 are now out. Professor in History was his third but second fictional book of a man who is an atheist but has the fantastic opportunity to ask Jesus unique questions on various topics. It chronicles the End of the Earth from a Biblical perspective in a fictional form.

Some of his books are fiction (*How He Lived an Undead Life* a story of horror in the second half of the Tribulation), and others are non-fiction (*The Wedding of Jesus: The Invitations have been Sent* a tale of the Sheep, Remnant, Goats and the Bride of Christ and how they are described in the New Testament). You can find his works on DrScottYoung.com and on his YouTube channel!

Made in United States
Troutdale, OR
10/23/2024

24087763R00086